MIND-BOGGLING
ANIMAL PUZZLES

A Treasury of Fabulous Facts, Secret Codes, Games, Mazes, and More!

Mind-Boggling Animal Puzzles is an original work, first published in 2019 by Fox Chapel Publishing Company, Inc. Reproduction of its contents is strictly prohibited without written permission from the rights holder.

ISBN 978-1-64124-044-4

To learn more about the other great books from Fox Chapel Publishing, or to find a retailer near you, call toll-free 800-457-9112 or visit us at *www.FoxChapelPublishing.com*.

We are always looking for talented authors. To submit an idea, please send a brief inquiry to acquisitions@foxchapelpublishing.com.

Fox Chapel Publishing makes every effort to use environmentally friendly paper for printing.

Printed in China
First printing

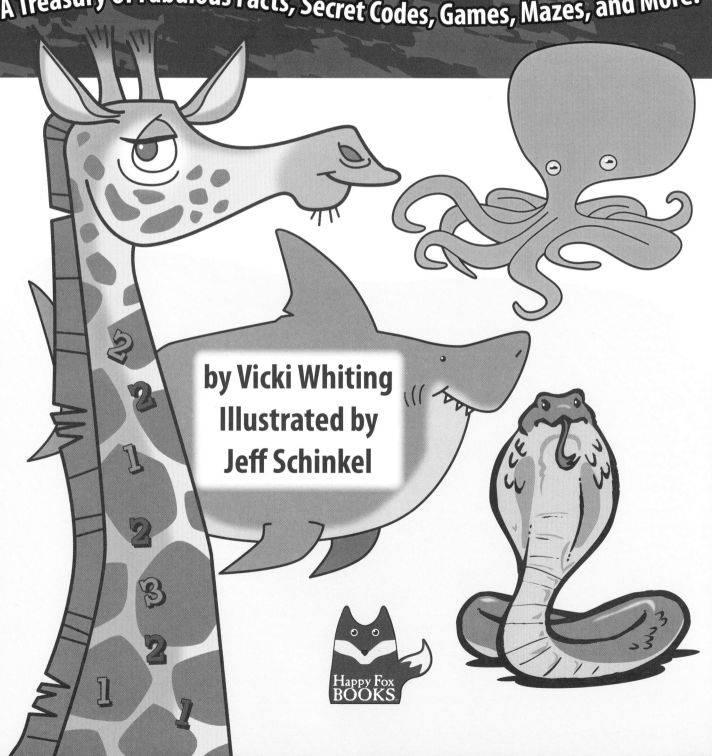

MIND-BOGGLING ANIMAL PUZZLES

A Treasury of Fabulous Facts, Secret Codes, Games, Mazes, and More!

by Vicki Whiting
Illustrated by
Jeff Schinkel

Kid Scoop

Happy Fox BOOKS

Contents

What do you call an alligator wearing a vest?

ANSWER: An investigator!

ARCTIC

Super-Duper Animal Facts!

Did you know...
...that a dog was once the King of Norway? That there are more than 150 species of octopus? That an anaconda can grow as long as a school bus?!

Read all about it here, all while doing fun challenges, answering riddles, following tricky mazes, finding clues, decoding mysterious secret messages, and solving puzzles.

Do you want to be even smarter than you are now?
Scientists have shown that doing the animal activities in this book boosts your knowledge and your brain power!

Turn the page and start your amazing journey to learn, play, and boost your brain!

Animal Jokes

Why did the elephant paint himself different colors?

ANSWER: So he could hide in the crayon box.

What does a cat say when it gets hurt?

ANSWER: "Me Ow!"

Why do hummingbirds hum?

ANSWER: Because they don't know the words.

What do you call an alligator wearing a vest?

ANSWER: An investigator!

What do you call a squid that can transform into a robot?

ANSWER: Octopus Prime

Why do tigers have stripes?

ANSWER: So they won't be spotted.

Why is it no fun to play basketball with pigs?

ANSWER: Because they always hog the ball.

Why are fish such terrible Ping-Pong players?

ANSWER: They don't like to get close to the net.

Food Friends

I f it weren't for honey bees, many of your favorite foods would disappear from the planet. In fact, honey bees **pollinate*** more crops than any other insect.

Circle every third letter along each bee's flight path below to discover just a few of the foods that busy honey bees pollinate.

* Pollinate means to move pollen between plants, allowing the plant to make seeds and reproduce.

R B A T R P J S P V W L T D E Z A S

P E O C D N M G I K A O Y W N K L S

W U P G H U L B M I O P J T K S D I L Y N O K S

S I C H I H M B E W V R T S R Z O I P L E A F S

BZZZzzzZZZzzz!

Bees stroke their wings 11,400 times per minute! That's what makes their distinctive buzzing sound.

Hooray for hairy legs!

Honey bees are actually fuzzy little insects. When one stops by a flower to sip some nectar, pollen gets stuck to its hairy body. When the busy bee moves on to another flower, it drops some pollen from the first flower onto the second flower. This allows flowers to make seeds, bear fruit, and reproduce.

We also **eat** pollen!

Can you find the bee twins?

Pollen Pathway

Help this honey bee find the correct path through the flowers as it collects pollen. You can move across, up, down, or diagonally. Add the numbers on each flower along your path. The correct path adds up to 21.

Start →

3	6	3	7
0	4	2	5
5	3	6	0
2	1	0	2

Finish ←

Dancing Directions

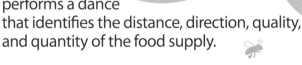

When a honey bee returns to its hive, it gives out samples of the flowers' nectar to its colony. Then it performs a dance that identifies the distance, direction, quality, and quantity of the food supply.

The round dance indicates that a food supply has been found. The waggle dance indicates the angle and distance of the food supply, telling the other bees how to get there.

Why do bees make honey?

Honey bees make honey so they have something to eat during the long months of the year when flowers aren't blooming.

Home Sweet Home

Honey bees live in groups called a **colony**. The place where the colony lives is called a **hive**. As many as 60,000 honey bees can live in one hive!

How many bees can you find on these two pages?

BUTTERFLIES

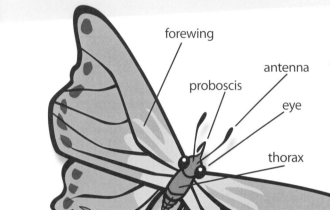

Labels: forewing, proboscis, antenna, eye, thorax, hindwing, abdomen

A World of Delight

It's a flower! It's a bird! It's a **butterfly!** While butterflies may look like flying flowers, they are living insects.

Scientists estimate that there are 12,000 to 15,000 species of butterflies in the world.

Butterflies can be found on all continents except one. Write the letter that comes before each letter below to reveal that continent.

$$\frac{A}{B} \ \overline{O} \ \overline{U} \ \overline{B} \ \overline{S} \ \overline{D} \ \overline{U} \ \overline{J} \ \overline{D} \ \overline{B}$$

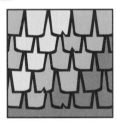

A butterfly has a coiled proboscis for drinking liquids such as flower nectar.

Butterfly wings are covered with colored scales.

A butterfly can fly at a top speed of

$$6 + 3 + 5 - 2 = \underline{\hspace{1cm}}$$

miles per hour.

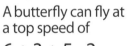

Moth or butterfly?

Butterflies are colorful insects with long, clubbed antennae that fly during the day. Moths fly at night and lack clubs at the end of their antennae. Some moths have antennae that look almost like feathers.

Are butterflies poisonous?

Some butterflies, such as the monarch and pipe-vine swallowtail, eat poisonous plants as caterpillars and are poisonous themselves as adult butterflies. Birds learn not to eat them.

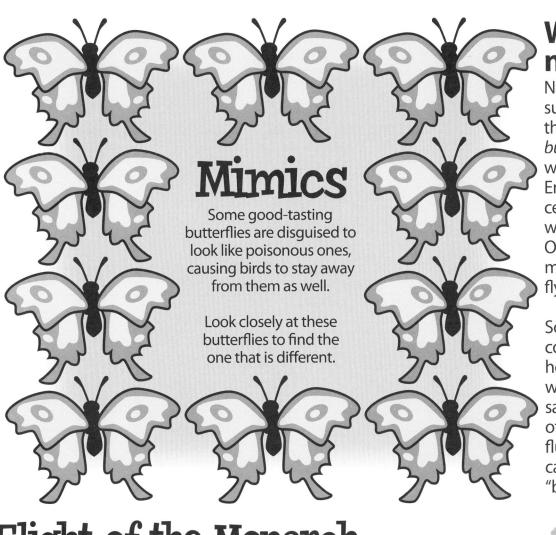

Mimics

Some good-tasting butterflies are disguised to look like poisonous ones, causing birds to stay away from them as well.

Look closely at these butterflies to find the one that is different.

What's in a name?

No one knows for sure why we call these insects *butterflies,* since the word has been in the English language for centuries (the word was *buterfleoge* in Old English, which means "butter and flying creature").

Some people think it comes from someone hearing "butterfly" when someone else said, "flutter-by." In other languages, the fluttery bug is not called anything like "butter" and "fly."

Flight of the Monarch

Replace the missing words.

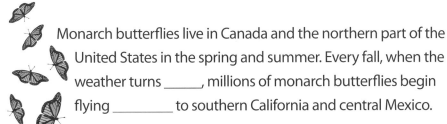

ONCE SOUTH KINGDOM COLD ORANGE RETURN

While quite small, the beautiful _____ and black monarch butterfly makes one of the longest migrations in the animal _____.

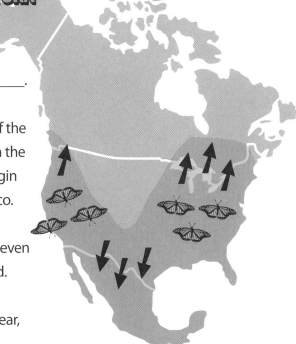

Monarch butterflies live in Canada and the northern part of the United States in the spring and summer. Every fall, when the weather turns _____, millions of monarch butterflies begin flying _____ to southern California and central Mexico.

The butterflies _____ to the same forests each year, and some even find the same tree where their parents and grandparents wintered.

Scientists aren't sure how the monarchs know where to go each year, since they each only make the trip _____.

CATS

Cats have pressure-sensitive hairs called **vibrissae.** These are the whiskers, eyebrows, and the long hair on the backs of their paws. This helps them "see" in the dark.

Purrr-fect Pets

Cats have been pets for people for thousands of years. They were taken in to help keep mice and snakes out of homes, farms, and businesses.

Cats also appear in all kinds of stories, from fairy tales to legends to comic strips.

Cats have retractable claws. That keeps them sharp!

Cat Prints

Just like fingerprints, this part of a cat's body has a pattern of ridges that is unique to that cat.

SENO

Unscramble the word to find the answer.

Use the code to discover some fun facts about cats.

0 =   4 =   7 =

2 =   5 =   8 =

3 =   6 =   9 =

The number of muscles in each ear of a cat.

The number of years ago that we believe cats were first tamed.

MILLION
The approximate number of dollars spent each year in the U.S. for kitty litter.

The approximate number of kittens born in the U.S. each day.

Are black cats really bad luck?

Some people believe that a black cat crossing their path is good luck. And some believe it is bad luck. These are called **superstitions**.

What you believe might depend on where you live. Many people in Britain and Japan think black cats are good luck. In Germany, some believe that black cats crossing a person's path from right to left is bad luck. But if the cat walks from left to right, they believe it brings good luck.

How many mice can you find on this page?

SUPERSTITION:
A belief that certain things or actions have the power to bring about good or bad luck.

Each black cat below has an exact twin except one. Can you find the unique black cat? Good luck!

Ancient Egyptians loved cats!

Egyptians considered cats to be sacred, which is why they mummified and buried them in tombs. They would honor a god by portraying it with a cat's head.

The Egyptian goddess Bast was shown with the head of a cat. Bast is the Egyptian goddess of sunrise and the protector of cats, women, and children.

Connect the dots in alphabetical order to draw Bast.

How many differences can you find between the two coyotes?

Prairie Predators

Coyotes live all over the United States, but most of them live in the western states.

Coyotes are very much like dogs. The puppies play with each other and wrestle like puppies. But when they're full grown, coyotes can be a big problem for ranchers.

Coyote Stretches

Get a little exercise and limber up the coyote way!

Coyote Stretch #1

Sit on your haunches and howl. Feel your neck stretch? Raise your shoulders up and down as you howl!

Coyote Stretch #2

Imitate the pose of this coyote. While on all fours, arch your back and stretch. Can you raise your arm?

Coyote Stretch #3

Roll on your back and wiggle your arms and legs in the air like you're rolling in the desert sand.

Coyote Stretch #4

Coyotes are amazing jumpers. Can you balance on all fours and jump up and down?

Complete the grid by using all the letters in the word HOWLS in each vertical and horizontal row. Each letter should only be used once in each row.

H	O	W	L	S
W	L			
	S		W	
		H		
O				H

The Legendary Coyote

The coyote plays a central role in Native American legends. Sometimes he appears as a **trickster** – someone who plays jokes and tricks in order to get what he needs. Sometimes he appears as a **creator**.

Read this Karok legend. Do you think the coyote in the legend is being a trickster, a creator, or both?

There once was a time when humans did not have fire to keep them warm. The only beings in the world that knew how to make fire were the Fire Beings.

Coyote, being the cleverest and slyest of all the Karok, decided to watch the Fire Beings and learn how to make fire.

The Fire Beings guarded the secret of fire very carefully. But when the Fire Beings' watch changed, Coyote grabbed the fire and ran. One of the Fire Beings chased after Coyote, but as we all know, coyotes are very fast. The Fire Beings grabbed only the tip of Coyote's tail, burning the fur. That is why coyotes have black tips on their tails.

There was a terrible tussle, but eventually Coyote threw the fire to Wood, who swallowed it and would not give it up to the Fire Beings again.

Coyote knew how to get the fire out of Wood, though – by simply rubbing two dry sticks together! And this, it is said, is how the Karok people learned how to create fire.

Read the Karok legend and number these pictures in order based on what you read.

Coyote Code

0 =	◺
1 =	◹
2 =	▤
3 =	▥
4 =	▤
5 =	▽
6 =	◉
7 =	◣
8 =	▣
9 =	◹

Discover some amazing coyote facts using the code at left.

Coyotes can jump over ◹▥ feet. That's higher than a basketball hoop, which is ◹◺ feet above the ground.

A coyote litter can have ▥ to ◹▤ pups.

Coyotes can run over ▤◺ miles per hour.

Coyotes live about ◹▤ years in the wild.

Coyotes can make ◹◹ different sounds.

CROCODILES

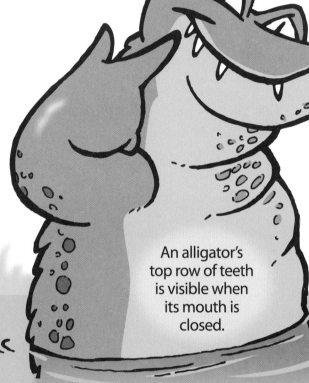

An alligator's top row of teeth is visible when its mouth is closed.

Crocs & Gators

Crocodiles and alligators look a lot alike. They are both reptiles from the order of animals named *Crocodylia*. But there are ways to tell them apart – from a safe distance, of course!

On crocodiles, some of the lower teeth stick up when their mouths are closed.

From above, an alligator's snout is U-shaped.

Don't bother trying to outrun a crocodile or an alligator. They have a swimming speed of 20 miles per hour (32 kph) and a running speed of 11 miles per hour (18 kph) for short distances.

A crocodile's snout is V-shaped.

How do crocodiles sweat?

Circle every other letter for the surprising answer!

T S H N E R Y P S D W M E J
A D T H T V H F R G O H U S
G Q H P T S H B E M I K R S
M T O P U L T W H V S C

Dangerous Neighbors

Crocodiles are potentially dangerous to humans. And they're carnivores, so they will catch and eat almost any creature they can. They don't chew and swallow, they just tear off chunks and swallow whole.

But humans are also dangerous to these creatures. Habitat destruction and over-hunting have made these ancient reptiles endangered species.

Hold the page up to a mirror to reveal this fascinating fact.

Crocodiles swallow stones to help them digest their food.

Pool of Facts **Use the secret code!**

The largest recorded alligator: 🔲⭕ feet long.

The largest recorded crocodile: ◼️🔺 feet long.

Alligators have ▨🔺 to 🔺🔺 teeth. They grow new ones to replace broken teeth. One alligator can have as many as ◼️🔺🔺🔺 teeth in a lifetime!

Crocs can stay underwater for 🔲◻️ to ◼️🔺 minutes. They close their nostrils when they swim underwater.

SECRET CODE

🔺 = 0	🔲 = 4	▨ = 7
🔳 = 1	🔻 = 5	🔺 = 8
◼️ = 2	◣ = 6	⭕ = 9

An American Original

The American alligator is the largest reptile in North America and has been here since the time of the dinosaurs – over 80 million years ago and it still looks the same.

Unscramble the letters to reveal the names of the two U.S. states where most American alligators live.

__ __ __ __ __ __ __ __
IOLASUANI

__ __ __ __ __ __ __
ODARLIF

DOGS & PUPPIES

Man's Best Friend

Dogs and people have been companions for about 20,000 years. Ancient cave paintings have been found showing dogs working alongside human hunters. Dogs have been trained to protect humans and livestock for centuries.

How many bones do you see?

Dog King

One dog was the King of Norway for three years when a past king returned to his country and gave his people a choice: "If you won't be ruled by me, pick this slave or this dog." The dog won!

Spot the Trail

Because Dalmatians were trained to run along with horses and carriages in the mid-1800s, they became known as carriage dogs. Their job was to scare other dogs that would chase the carriage and frighten the horses. Fire departments also used Dalmatians to guard their carriages. The Dalmatian became the mascot of the fire service.

Help the Dalmatian find her way to the fire.

Death Detectors

In ancient Greece, doctors used dogs to determine whether a person was dead or in a coma. A wag of the dog's tail would indicate life, but a motionless dog meant the person was most likely dead.

Hold this cartoon up to a mirror to read it.

Relax, pal! I was just taking a nap!

Puppy Tales

Tell a tale about a puppy. Be sure to tell details like the puppy's name, where it lives, what it looks like, and what it does. You can start your tale with "Once upon a time …"

Name That Breed

1. You can count on me as a true friend anytime, anyplace. I often work as a guide dog for the blind or physically disabled, a search and rescue dog, or as a dog who sniffs out illegal drugs.

I am strongly built and muscular in the hindquarters. I have a short, thick, water-resistant coat that is black, yellow, or chocolate colored. My tail is wide at the base, tapers to a point, and is covered with thick, short hair.

What breed am I?

A. Labrador Retriever

B. English Cocker Spaniel

C. Dachshund

2. I descended from various old breeds of German herding and farm dogs. I am the world's leading guard, police, and military dog. My courage, steadfast heart, and keen senses have endeared me to mankind.

My coat is harsh and medium length. I shed a lot, so I need to be brushed every other day, year round. My coat is usually tan with a black muzzle and a "saddle" over my back and sides.

What breed am I?

A. Belgian Sheepdog

B. German Shepherd

3. I am considered the national dog of France, although I originated in Germany where hunters commonly used me as a water retriever as far back as the fifteenth century. The pompom on my tail rose above the water so hunters could see me while I swam.

My topcoat is thick and curly. My undercoat is wooly and warm. My coat doesn't shed much, but it requires daily brushing and professional grooming.

A. Poodle   B. Lhasa Apso   C. Collie

What breed am I?

ELEPHANTS

How Many Elephants?

Elephants are the largest land animals in the world. But not all elephants are the same. Most scientists divide elephants into two main groups: **African** elephants and **Asian** elephants.

Some scientists believe grassland and forest elephants of Africa are so different that there should be *three* groups of elephants – Asian and two groups of African elephants.

African elephant

AFRICAN ELEPHANTS
Height: 10 feet (3 m)
Weight: 12,000 lbs (5,443 kg)

ASIAN ELEPHANTS
Height: 9 feet (2.75 m)
Weight: 10,000 lbs (4,535 kg)

Replace the missing words to learn more about African and Asian elephants.

WRINKLED   HOT   LARGER
AFRICA   COOL

African Elephants

African elephants are _____ than Asian elephants. They have large ears shaped a little like the continent of _____ . Large ears help keep the elephant _____ on the _____ African plains. African elephants have a swayback and very _____ skin. They also have a rounded head without any bumps.

EAT   BACKS   HIGH
COOLER   SMALLER

Asian Elephants

Asian elephants live in _____ forest areas and they have _____ ears. They also have rounded _____, smoother skin, and a _____ forehead with two "bumps." Asian elephants can _____ more than 300 pounds (136 kg) of grass, leaves, and plant material every day.

Pachyderm Patterns

An elephant, also known as a **pachyderm**, has skin that is rough and wrinkled. In fact, the creases in the lower part of their legs can be used to tell elephants apart. Like fingerprints, every elephant has its very own crease pattern.

Draw the picture that should come next to continue the pattern in each row.

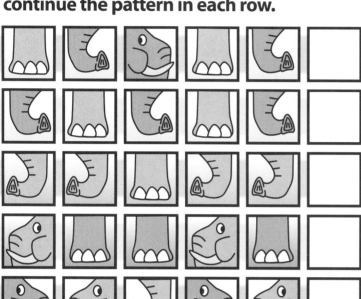

Asian elephant

Trunk Truths

One of these four statements is false. Which one?

1. The first elephants appeared about 50 million years ago. The first elephant, called Moeritherium (meer-uh-THEER-ee-um), was only about 2 feet (0.6 m) tall and had no trunk.

2. Asian elephants have one small "finger" at the end of their trunks for grasping. African elephants have two "fingers."

Asian

African

3. Elephants' trunks contain bones similar to the human spine.

4. There are more than 100,000 muscles in the trunk, making it very flexible and strong enough to lift whole trees.

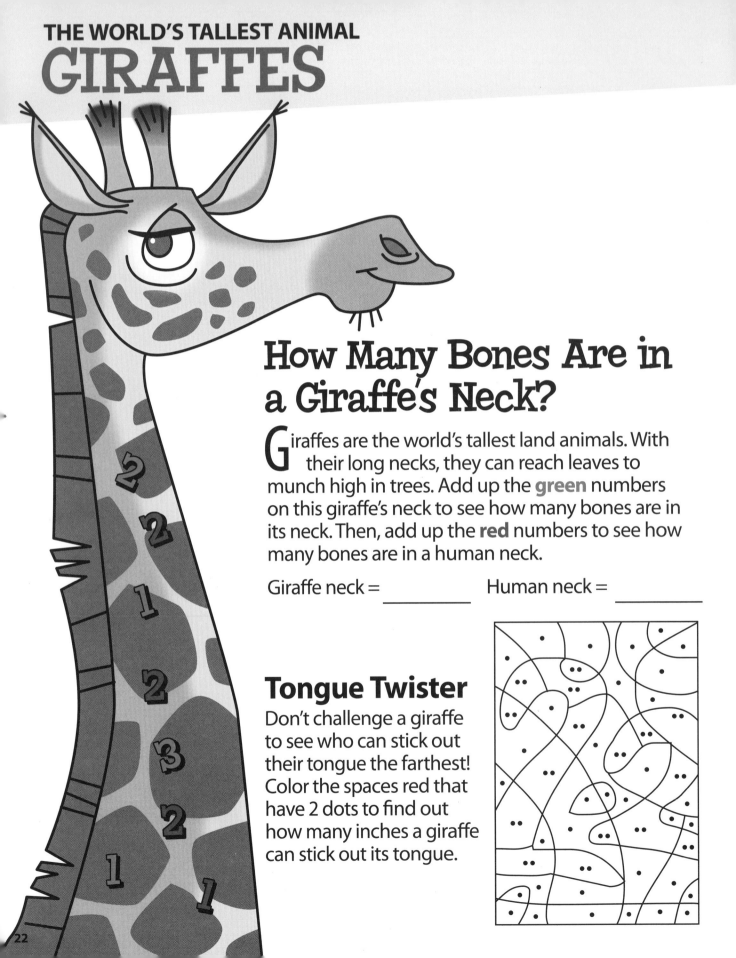

How Many Bones Are in a Giraffe's Neck?

Giraffes are the world's tallest land animals. With their long necks, they can reach leaves to munch high in trees. Add up the **green** numbers on this giraffe's neck to see how many bones are in its neck. Then, add up the **red** numbers to see how many bones are in a human neck.

Giraffe neck = _____   Human neck = _____

Tongue Twister

Don't challenge a giraffe to see who can stick out their tongue the farthest! Color the spaces red that have 2 dots to find out how many inches a giraffe can stick out its tongue.

How Do Giraffes Sleep?

A long, deep sleep is very dangerous for a giraffe. They might not sense when a predator comes near.

During the day, giraffes doze on and off for a few minutes at a time. Quietly and gently, they relax their necks and let their heads hang downward.

At night, they lie down. But even then, they only take cat naps. To watch for danger, they wake up every few minutes to look around before taking another short nap.

FINISH

How tall is a giraffe?
Find the missing number to find out how tall a giraffe grows.

$$2 + \rule{2cm}{0.4pt} = 18 \text{ feet}$$

That is the size of three to four grown men standing on each other's shoulders!

Male giraffes are slightly taller than females.

Baby giraffes are about 6 feet (2 m) tall when they are born. Within about 10 hours, the baby giraffe will be running around.

START

A flea is bothering this giraffe. Guide the flea through the maze to leave the poor giraffe alone.

DOUBLE WORD SEARCH

Find these words in the word search puzzle. Then look for them on these two pages.

GIRAFFE	GROW	ANIMALS
TALL	LEAVES	FLEA
REACH	ADULT	TONGUE
BABY	FEMALE	LAND
NECK	NIGHT	STICK
SLEEP	DAY	DANGER

```
J G S W M R N O S L A M I N A T
P R T B A B Y E N R D X C U A P
S O I Y A D E T I S A Q B L O R
Z W C U K L U F G T N S L E E P
Q S K C A S T L H L G A K A P D
W P E M T T J E T N E P C V N J
V N E K V L S A W E R H N E R D
E F F A R I G T O N G U E S V W
```

GORILLAS

5' 6"
5'
4' 6"
4'
3' 6"
3'
2' 6"
2'
1' 6"
1'
6"
0

Gorilla Facts

When a male gorilla is fully grown, he will start to grow silvery hair on his back, in the shape of a saddle. This is why we call them **silverback** gorillas.

Adult gorillas can weigh up to 400 pounds (181 kg), and when they stand on their two legs, are about 5.5 feet (1.7 m) tall.

How tall are you? Measure yourself, then mark your height next to the gorilla's height.

	GORILLA	ME
WEIGHT	400 lbs.	
HEIGHT	5' 6"	

Gorilla Troops

Replace the missing words using the list at right.

Gorillas like to be around other gorillas, so they live in _____, called troops, as one big gorilla family. A troop can _____ more than 30 gorillas, led by one or more silverback gorillas. These leaders _____ where the troop will live, and when it will wake up, _____, and go back to bed. They also make sure that no troop member _____ another.

INCLUDE
DECIDE   EAT
GROUPS   HURTS

How much do gorillas eat?

Along with their families, silverback gorillas are mostly herbivorous, which means that they usually eat vegetables and fruits.

A silverback gorilla can eat up to 45 pounds (20 kg) of food a day. That's about the weight of the items on this page that add up to 45. Do the math!

$8 + 4 =$

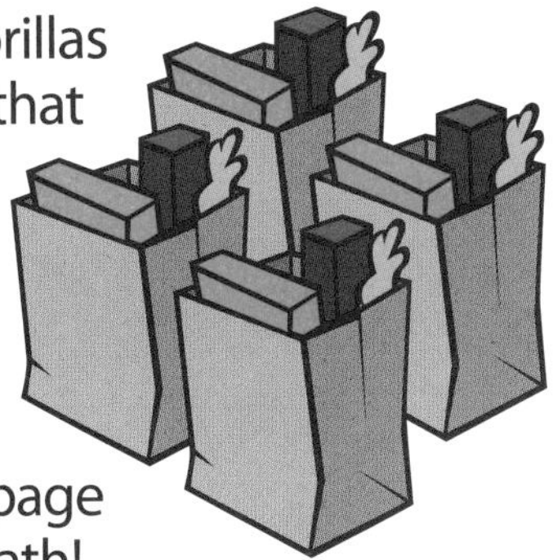

$23 + 11 + 11 =$

$18 + 18 + 9 =$

$7 + 9 - 4 =$

$19 - 8 =$

$28 - 19 =$

$12 + 24 + 9 =$

Connect the dots to draw a gorilla.

25

HERMIT CRABS

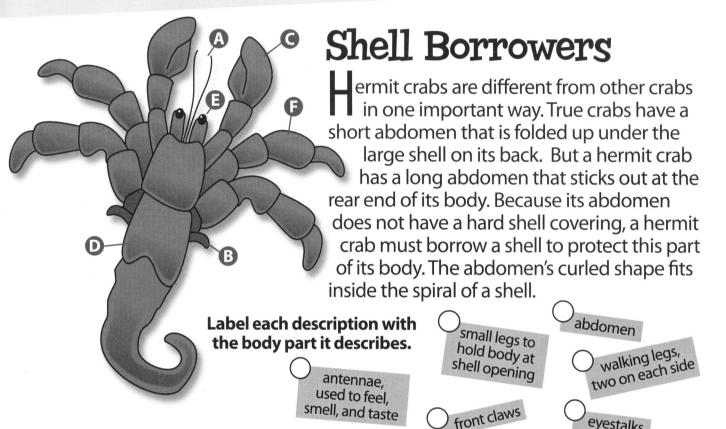

Shell Borrowers

Hermit crabs are different from other crabs in one important way. True crabs have a short abdomen that is folded up under the large shell on its back. But a hermit crab has a long abdomen that sticks out at the rear end of its body. Because its abdomen does not have a hard shell covering, a hermit crab must borrow a shell to protect this part of its body. The abdomen's curled shape fits inside the spiral of a shell.

Label each description with the body part it describes.

- small legs to hold body at shell opening
- abdomen
- walking legs, two on each side
- antennae, used to feel, smell, and taste
- front claws
- eyestalks

Anybody Home?

This growing hermit crab is feeling cramped. He has outgrown the old borrowed shell he has been living in and is looking for a new home. When he finds an empty shell, he uses his claws to check out the size.

If the size of the new shell is just right, he cleans the shell carefully. Then, he will quickly pull his abdomen out of the old shell and stick it into the new one. Home sweet home! (Until he grows larger and needs to move to a bigger shell, that is!)

Which shell will the hermit crab choose?

Do the math. The hermit crab will select the shell with numbers that add up to an even number.

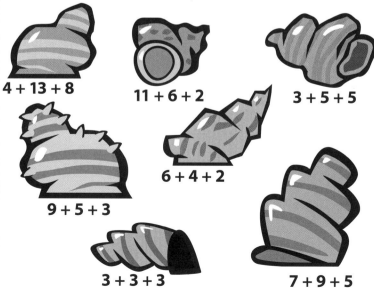

4 + 13 + 8

11 + 6 + 2

3 + 5 + 5

9 + 5 + 3

6 + 4 + 2

3 + 3 + 3

7 + 9 + 5

Hermit Crab's Baby Book

Which picture goes with each sentence telling how a hermit crab grows?

1. Mother hermit crab carries eggs inside the shell.

2. Mother hermit crab releases eggs that are ready to hatch into the ocean.

3. The hermit crab larva has large, bulging eyes and a long, shrimp-like body.

4. After its third molt, the hermit crab looks more like an adult hermit crab and will move closer to the shore and find a shell home.

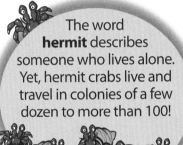

The word **hermit** describes someone who lives alone. Yet, hermit crabs live and travel in colonies of a few dozen to more than 100!

Molting

Both as a larva and an adult, a hermit crab grows by molting. A hermit crab has a hard outer covering called an exoskeleton. This covering doesn't grow like human skin. Instead, it must be shed when a new, larger exoskeleton is ready. The new exoskeleton is soft at first, and the hermit crab must stay inside its shell until it hardens.

Find the hermit crab twins.

Colorful Fliers

Have you ever watched a hummingbird flying by and noticed that their feathers seem to change color as they move into different light? Hummingbird feathers are **iridescent**, meaning that reflections of light make them appear different colors. Some hummingbirds are more colorful than others. Male hummingbirds are usually more colorful than females because they need to attract a mate. The females tend to camouflage (blend in) better with their nesting spots.

Find the differences between these two hummingbirds.

Hungry, Hungry Hummingbirds

Hummingbirds have an incredibly fast metabolism so they need to eat all day long. One hummingbird can eat up to twice its body weight and feed on hundreds of flowers in a single day.

If humans had a metabolism as fast as a hummingbird's, we'd need to eat more than 1,500 of these every day:
(circle every third letter)

JS**B**VWATBNESADKNMZAPRS

Use the code to learn more about hummingbirds.

■ = A ◤ = B ◹ = E ▮ = F ◣ = G

■ = I ▮ = L ◢ = N ◤ = P ◥ = Y

The ruby-throated hummingbird weighs less than a

___ ___ ___ ___ ___

The smallest hummingbird lives in Peru and is the size of a

___ ___ ___

Do hummingbirds hum? Yes! Their wings make a faint humming sound when they are

___ ___ ___ ___ ___ ___

Draw what comes next in each row to continue each pattern.

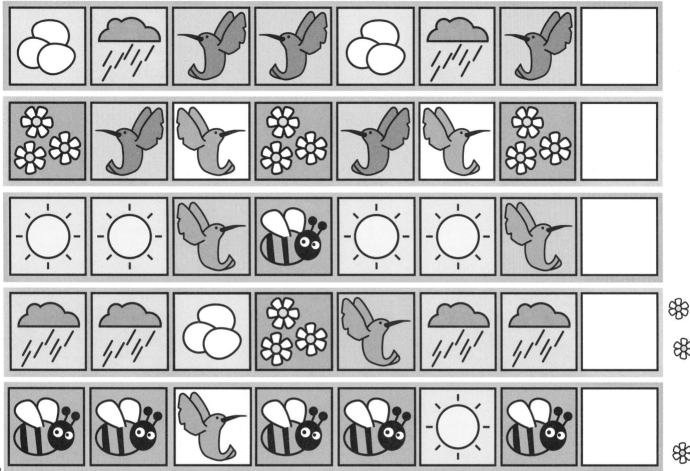

Fluttering Facts

How many hummingbirds and flowers can you find on these two pages?

Replace the missing words to learn more about hummingbirds.

 **SUMMER** **CONTINUOUS** **DIRECTION** **POLLEN** **JELLY BEANS** **FLOWERS**

Hummingbirds are the only birds that can fly in any _____: forward, backward, up, down, and side-to-side.

Hummingbirds pollinate flowers because _____ sticks to their wings. This feeding behavior is vital to helping _____ become pollinated, which makes hummingbirds very important to the ecosystem.

During migration, ruby-throated hummingbirds fly nonstop over

the Gulf of Mexico – it can take up to 22 hours of _____ flight over 500 miles (805 km) of water. The rufous hummingbird has the longest migration, traveling up to 6,000 miles (9,700 km) from its winter home to its

_____

breeding grounds.

Hummingbirds' nests and eggs are tiny. The eggs are about the size of _____. The nest is about the size of a walnut.

29

KANGAROOS

Marsupial Mamas

Kangaroos are **marsupials**, which means they are mammals that have an external pouch or pocket. Marsupials are different from most mammals because they give birth to very underdeveloped young. **Joeys** are born hairless and tiny, about the size of a bean and must climb their way up into their mother's pouch. They remain here to feed and sleep and grow – in six months they grow to be 2,000 times the size they were at birth.

Where can kangaroos be found? Solve each math problem to label the map.

| 32 - 11 = AUSTRALIA |
| 16 + 16 = NEW ZEALAND |
| 29 - 6 = PAPUA NEW GUINEA |

23

Indonesia

Pacific Ocean

21

Indian Ocean

32

Roo Features

Replace the missing words.

SENSES   STEER

HEARING   LARGE

SUPPORT

A kangaroo, or roo, has _____ back legs, small front legs, and a head shaped like that of a deer. Its well-developed _____ include excellent scanning eyesight and sharp _____ provided by large rabbit-like ears that can turn frontward or back. In a larger roo, the tail acts as a _____ for sitting, but also helps the animal _____ when hopping. Powerful back legs propel larger roos to speeds of up to 40 mph (64 kph).

World-Famous Jumpers

Their strong back legs launch kangaroos into the air. And their tails help them balance, as they hop great distances. When they hop, kangaroos use only their hind legs, which move together, much like those of a rabbit.

MEASURING BAR (Each stripe = 1 foot [0.3 m])

Rabbit　　**Gray Kangaroo**　　**Red Kangaroo**

Hopping Contest

Stand in one spot with your feet together. Now make a giant hop. How far did you hop? Mark that distance on the above grid. Look how far a gray roo, a red roo, and a rabbit can hop. How do you compare?

• •

Draw a line from each question to the answer that makes the most sense.

Which is the smallest kangaroo?

How many different kinds of kangaroos are there?

Which is the largest kangaroo?

More than 60 species.

The red kangaroo is around 175 lbs (80 kg).

The musky rat-kangaroo is less than a pound (0.5 kg).

What do you call a lazy kangaroo?

ANSWER: A pouch potato.

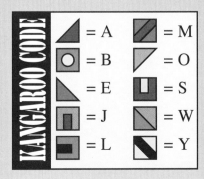
31

KOALAS

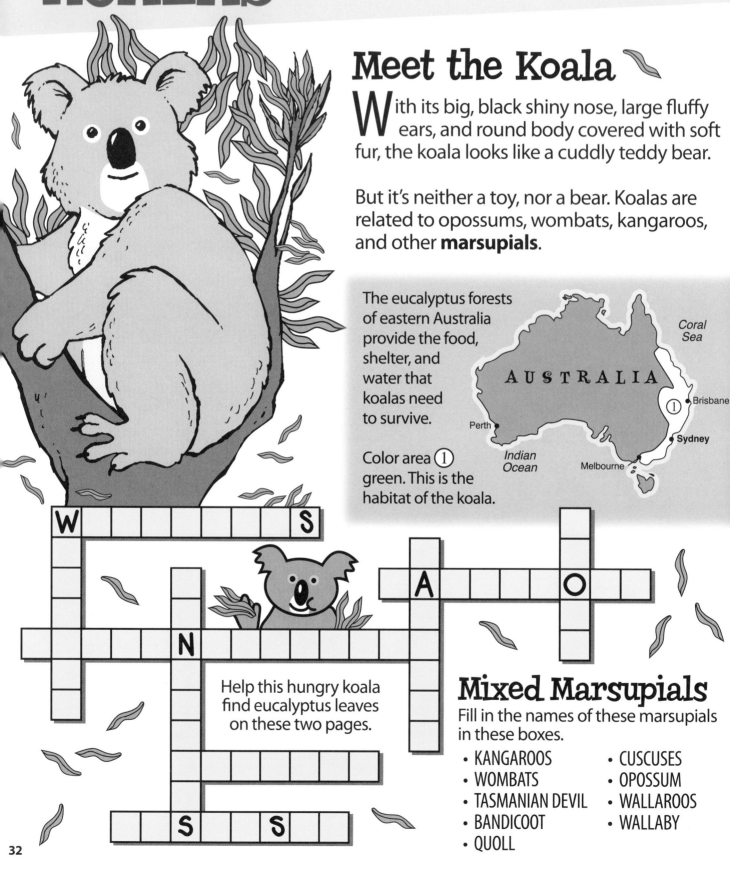

Meet the Koala

With its big, black shiny nose, large fluffy ears, and round body covered with soft fur, the koala looks like a cuddly teddy bear.

But it's neither a toy, nor a bear. Koalas are related to opossums, wombats, kangaroos, and other **marsupials**.

The eucalyptus forests of eastern Australia provide the food, shelter, and water that koalas need to survive.

Color area ① green. This is the habitat of the koala.

AUSTRALIA

Coral Sea

Perth

Indian Ocean

Brisbane

Sydney

Melbourne

Help this hungry koala find eucalyptus leaves on these two pages.

Mixed Marsupials

Fill in the names of these marsupials in these boxes.

- KANGAROOS
- WOMBATS
- TASMANIAN DEVIL
- BANDICOOT
- QUOLL
- CUSCUSES
- OPOSSUM
- WALLAROOS
- WALLABY

Ahhhh... Naptime!

Koalas are nocturnal, which means they sleep during the day and are active at night. Koalas sleep about 18 hours each day.

Koalas don't build nests or platforms. When they get sleepy, they find a nice cozy fork in the tree branches. Though the hard branches of a tree wouldn't seem comfortable to us, the koala has a thick layer of fat and fur on its behind – its own built-in cushion!

Which two sleepy koalas are exactly alike?

KOALA CODE

1 = ◿
2 = ▥
3 = ◺
4 = ▣
5 = ▽
6 = ▤
7 = ▤
8 = △
9 = ▽
0 = ◸

Koalas eat about

____ pounds (1 kg)
◩

of leaves every day.

That's about ____%
▱▱

of a koala's weight.

In the wild, koalas

live about _____
◳ ◹

years.

Koalas sleep

about _____
◿ ◹

hours a day.

An adult koala weighs about

_____ pounds (14 kg).
◳ ◹

Feet Made for Tree Climbing

Replace the missing words.

| GRIP | USED | HOLDING | ROUND |

A koala's claws are just right for _____ onto tree trunks and branches. The front paws have five toes: two on one side of the foot and three on the other. That's like having two thumbs, an arrangement that gives the koala a strong _____.

The toes on the back paws are different from those on the front. In back, there's a _____ "big toe" without a claw, plus three other toes, two of which are joined to form one digit with two claws. These joined toes are _____ for grooming.

FRONT PAW

BACK PAW

33

Start

Finish

King of the Beasts?

Since ancient times, the size and strength of lions have so impressed people that these big cats became known as the "king of the jungle." But lions don't live in the jungle. They live on the grasslands of Africa known as **savannahs**.

Lions are one of the world's largest cats. A full-grown male lion can weigh from 330 to 550 pounds (150-250 kg). The average human male weighs about 160 pounds (73 kg).

Lion Lie Detector

After reading each statement about lions below, do each math problem. If your answer is an even number, that statement is TRUE. If the answer is an odd number, the statement is FALSE.

Lion cubs have spots. **12 + 4 =**

Lions are herbivores. **17 - 6 =**

In the wild, lions can go a week without eating. **9 + 9 =**

A full-grown lion can eat 75 pounds (34 kg) of meat at one time. **14 + 6 =**

Lions have five legs. **5 + 8 =**

A group of lions is called a pride. **23 + 3 =**

Find all the words hidden in the word search.

SAVANNAH
MAMMAL
ROAR
MANE
PRIDE
CUBS
TAIL
GAZELLE
GRASS
AFRICA
TEETH
RUN

S	T	B	Y	W	J	N	X	G	P	D
W	D	E	T	V	L	T	B	R	L	X
Q	R	S	E	A	D	R	M	W	R	B
Z	L	D	M	T	J	B	N	A	E	N
N	I	M	Y	Q	H	G	R	A	S	S
H	A	N	N	A	V	A	S	K	A	S
M	T	X	H	H	D	Z	K	H	C	T
F	S	T	G	J	B	E	P	E	I	L
G	T	B	T	L	G	L	R	W	R	N
H	H	N	U	Y	R	L	I	O	F	E
J	U	V	F	C	T	E	D	G	A	M
R	M	W	M	M	A	N	E	C	S	R

Open Wide!

A lion's teeth are made for eating meat. They have four pointed canine teeth that they use to kill prey and to tear off bites to eat. They have no molars or teeth for chewing. They swallow bites of food whole!

Use the grid to help you complete the drawing of the lion above. Then color it!

Hide and Seek

Lion cubs are easy prey for other carnivores. A special camouflage helps to keep them safe. The golden tan of a cub's fur and the dark brown of the spots blend in with the light and shadow of the grassy savannah.

How many lion cubs can you spot hiding in the grass below?

Look-Alike Lions: Can you find the two lions that are identical?

35

OCTOPUSES

Mysterious Loners

There are more than 150 species of octopuses, all with eight tentacles. These soft-bodied invertebrates (animals without a backbone) range in size. One species is no bigger than your thumb, while the Pacific giant octopus grows to be 10 feet or more (3 m or more) from the tip of one tentacle to another and can weigh up to 50 pounds (23 kg).

The life of an octopus is one of constant peril. Crabs and small fish like to dine on their eggs and young. And a grown octopus must always watch out for other predators in the sea.

Trouble? Think Ink!

To escape from a predator, an octopus will squirt out a dark cloud of ink. Thousands of feet down, where the sea is already inky black, they squirt a glow-in-the-dark ink.

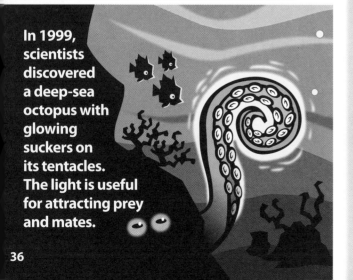

In 1999, scientists discovered a deep-sea octopus with glowing suckers on its tentacles. The light is useful for attracting prey and mates.

Eight Arms or Legs?

An octopus has eight arms ... or are they legs? Scientists think two of the limbs act as legs, and the rest are more like arms.

Octopuses can change their body shape. The only solid part of their body is the skull. If the skull can squeeze through a hole, the octopus can pull its entire body through that hole. This can be a problem for aquariums.

Colorful Characters

Usually, an octopus is brown. But if it gets angry or scared, it changes color depending upon its mood. And it can also change colors to blend in with rocks, coral, sand, and more. This is called **camouflage** (kam-O-flawj).

Color each little octopus so it matches the background and can hide.

How many fish can you find on this page in two minutes?

Predator Problems

The most deadly predator for an octopus is the moray eel. It can slip into the same crevice where the octopus hides. Its strong jaws can easily tear off an octopus's tentacle!

If an octopus loses a tentacle, it can grow a replacement.

Can you find the octopus at right that has only seven tentacles?

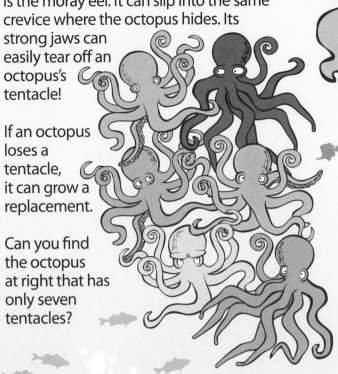

Can you follow the inky trail to help this octopus find her cave?

ORCAS

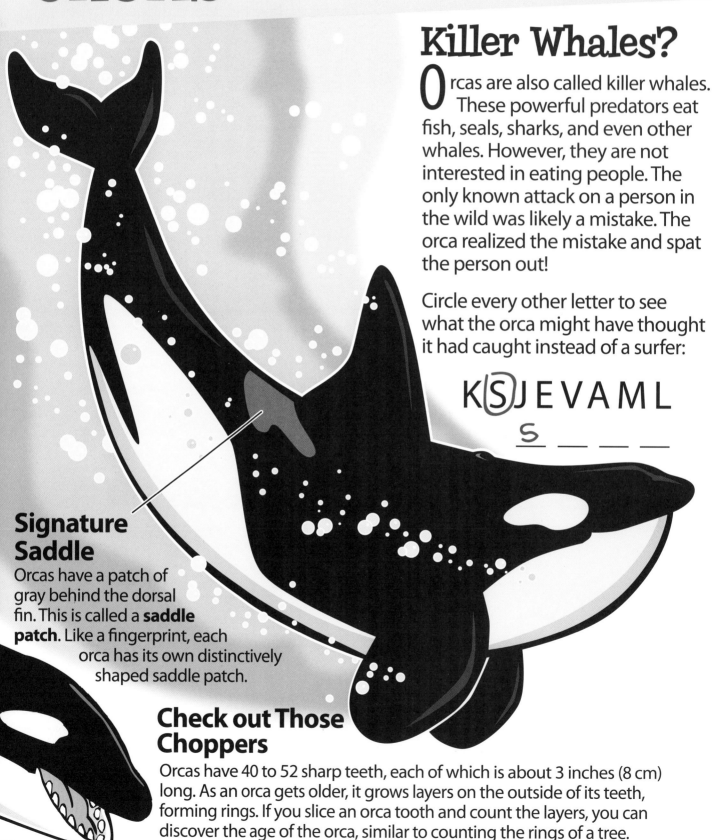

Killer Whales?

Orcas are also called killer whales. These powerful predators eat fish, seals, sharks, and even other whales. However, they are not interested in eating people. The only known attack on a person in the wild was likely a mistake. The orca realized the mistake and spat the person out!

Circle every other letter to see what the orca might have thought it had caught instead of a surfer:

K S J E V A M L

S _ _ _ _

Signature Saddle

Orcas have a patch of gray behind the dorsal fin. This is called a **saddle patch**. Like a fingerprint, each orca has its own distinctively shaped saddle patch.

Check out Those Choppers

Orcas have 40 to 52 sharp teeth, each of which is about 3 inches (8 cm) long. As an orca gets older, it grows layers on the outside of its teeth, forming rings. If you slice an orca tooth and count the layers, you can discover the age of the orca, similar to counting the rings of a tree.

Camo Colors

From the land, the orca's black and white pattern may not look like good camouflage. But it is, and it helps the orca sneak up on its prey.

As an orca is swimming in the deep ocean, the fish swimming above it look down and see only darkness.

Fish swimming below an orca look up and see the white of the orca's underbody, which blends with the bright light of the sun shining down through the water.

Male orcas can reach up to 30 feet (9 m) long and weigh as much as 7 tons or 14,000 pounds (6,350 kg). That's nearly as big as a:

5 6 3 8 8 4

9 1 5

ORCA CODE:

B=9	L=4	T=2
C=6	O=8	U=1
H=3	S=5	Z=7

Which of these statements about orcas are true? The answers that are true add up to even numbers.

Orcas lay eggs.
19 + 8 − 2 =

Orcas feed milk to their babies.
9 + 9 + 4 =

Orcas are warm-blooded.
17 + 6 + 3 =

Orcas give birth to live young.
10 + 9 + 5 =

Orcas have hair.
15 + 5 − 3 =

Orcas have scales.
8 + 6 + 5 =

HINT: Orcas are mammals, just like people.

Can you find the two identical orcas?

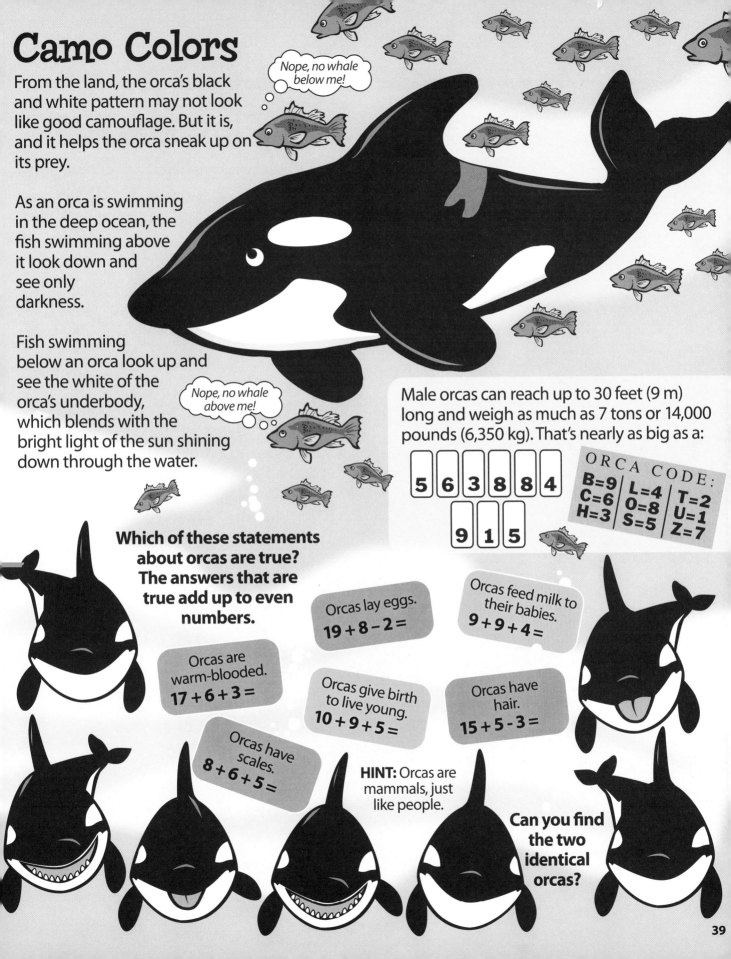

39

PANDAS

Are Pandas Bears?

A couple of decades ago, scientists determined that giant pandas are most closely related to bears, although they are also a lot like raccoons.

Pandas are different from other bears. For one thing, they have eyes like a cat. And their front paws have an unusual thumb – sometimes called a false thumb. It's part of the wrist bone and sticks out to the side like an extra finger.

Panda eye

Bear eye

Always Hungry

Giant pandas eat day and night, constantly wandering through the forest eating and eating. Add up the numbers along the correct path of the maze to find out how many pounds of food one giant panda can eat in a day.

Start

Big Mama

A mother panda is about 800 times heavier than her baby. (If a human mother with a 7-pound baby weighed 800 times more, she would weigh 5,600 pounds. That's nearly 3 tons!)

3 2 5 4 5 5 3 5 6 9 8 7 1 POUNDS 5 2 8 7

While bamboo makes up most of a giant panda's diet, pandas sometimes eat small animals. Because of this small amount of meat eating, giant pandas are classified as carnivores.

Pandas Big and Small

The largest giant pandas can weigh about 250 pounds (113 kg). Ask five friends how much they weigh. Add up their weights. Does it equal 250 pounds?

Baby pandas are itty-bitty bears. They weigh only 4 to 6 ounces (113-170 g) at birth.

Number the pandas in order from smallest to biggest.

Endangered Pandas

Because of its distinctive features and its status as endangered, the giant panda was chosen by the world's largest conservation organization as a symbol of conservation.

Use these four missing letters to fill in the blanks to discover the name of the organization. They can be used more than once.

| W | L | F | D |

_ O R _ _   _ I _ _ _ I _ E   _ U N _

Where to See Pandas

About 300 giant pandas live in zoos and research centers worldwide. Threatened with extinction, these captive breeding programs are seen as hope for the giant panda's survival.

How many pandas can you find on this page?

All giant pandas and their cubs are on loan from China.

Agreements between these zoos and the Chinese conservation organizations are helping to preserve this endangered species.

Do the math to find out the number of giant pandas in each of these zoos in America and Canada.

San Diego Zoo

$9+8-14 =$ _____

Toronto Zoo

$17+23-38 =$ _____

Smithsonian National Zoo, Washington, D.C.

$14+8-18 =$ _____

Zoo Atlanta

$38-19-15 =$ _____

Memphis Zoo

$22-13-7 =$ _____

POLAR BEARS

Very Special Fur

Polar bears have two types of fur: long oily hairs and short insulating hairs.

The long, oily guard hairs are tiny, hollow tubes that trap warmth and hold it close to the skin. Their oily surface keeps polar bears dry.

Under the guard hairs is a layer of dense, short, soft hairs that trap heat close to the skin, like thermal underwear.

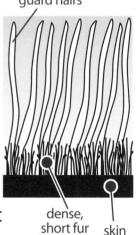

guard hairs

dense, short fur

skin

Polar Bear Fur Is NOT White!

Each polar bear hair shaft is transparent (clear). It has a hollow core that scatters and reflects visible light, much like what happens with ice and snow, giving it a bright white appearance.

How Polar Bears Stay Warm

Polar bears live on ice near the North Pole in the Arctic, which is covered in ice and surrounded by very cold water. But that doesn't bother a polar bear.

In each box, write the letter that comes before the letter at the bottom of each box to find a couple of cool ways these fluffy fellows stay warm.

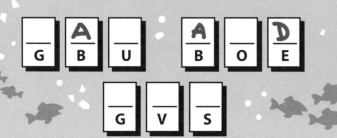

_	A	_		A	_	D
G	B	U		B	O	E

_	_	_
G	V	S

ARCTIC

ANTARCTICA

Movies and books sometimes show polar bears and penguins together. But they actually live on opposite ends of the earth. Polar bears only live in the Arctic and penguins live in Antarctica.

Polar Bear Paws

Polar bear paws can grow to be 12 inches (31 cm) across. They help distribute weight when treading on thin ice.

When swimming, their broad forepaws act like large paddles and the hind paws serve as rudders for steering.

Black footpads on the bottom of each paw are covered by small, soft bumps known as papillae. Papillae grip the ice and keep the bear from slipping. Their claws and tufts of fur between their toes and footpads may also help them grip the ice.

Polar Bear True or False

These statements are either all TRUE or all FALSE. Check your answers by adding up the numbers next to each of your answers. If the total is 33, you've got it right!

A polar bear's nose can smell a seal on the ice 20 miles (32 km) away!
❑ TRUE (5)
❑ FALSE (9)

Polar bear cubs are born without hair and are blind and deaf.
❑ TRUE (16)
❑ FALSE (7)

Polar bear young are called cubs.
❑ TRUE (10)
❑ FALSE (8)

Polar bear skin is black.
❑ TRUE (2)
❑ FALSE (12)

POLAR	D	S	W	T	L	S	N	A	P	O	A
BEAR	S	W	I	M	C	N	G	Q	F	A	S
ICE	N	A	S	V	R	T	B	E	I	B	W
SNOW	O	P	M	C	F	L	N	W	S	R	I
FUR	W	O	L	N	U	E	I	Z	H		
PAWS	J	L	P	M	R	B	K	C	J		
SWIM	P	A	T	V	M	D	S	R	E		
CUBS	S	R	A	E	B	F	K	C			
SKIN	C	L	A	W	S	G	I				
FISH	V	D	G	A							
CLAWS	B	H	R								

What's another name for a polar bear's layer of fat? The letters along the correct ice path reveal the answer.

START

B N E
A E
Z C L
R
B T
U
E B
R END

Write the answer here:

L ☐ ☐ ☐ E ☐

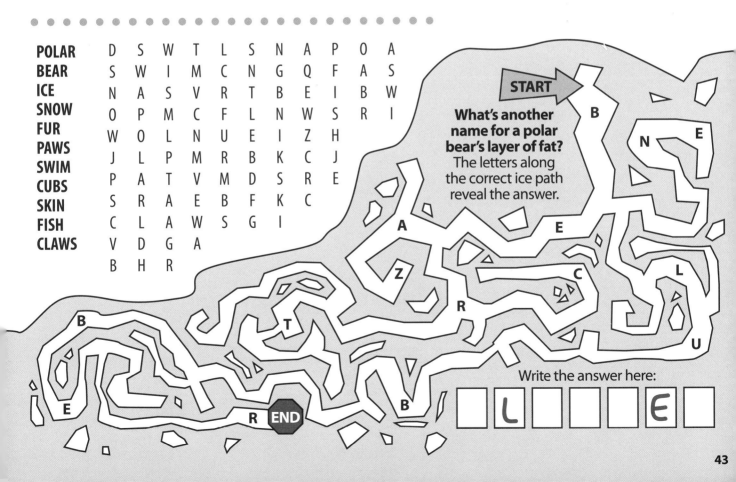

You Dirty Rat!

Rats have a dirty reputation. But, in reality, they like to wash themselves often and keep clean.

However, a rat in the wild can bite and can carry dangerous diseases. *Never try to catch one!*

Find the differences between these two rats.

Replace the words this rat chewed out of the paragraphs below:

GNAW TEETH WIRING INCHES FARMS CAUSE DIE

Rats Have Expensive Taste

From the day it is born, a rat's _____ never stop growing. They can grow up to five _____ a year. Rats must continue to _____ on hard surfaces to wear down their teeth or they will _____.

Rats can chew through walls, _____, plastic, and more. It is estimated that rats _____ about $20 billion in damage to homes, _____ , and businesses in the United States each year.

Mighty Mouths

Rats have been known to gnaw through iron cabinets and even concrete to get food!

Hold this paragraph up to a mirror to reveal a surprising rat fact:

Rats can bite down with a force of 7,000 pounds per square inch. That's about the same force as a crocodile's bite!

Rats bite thousands of people every year. They tend to bite only when cornered. However, dogs bite about 3 million people per year. Rats seldom carry rabies.

Big Appetites

Rats eat about ⅒ of their body weight every day. That would be like you eating about 20 pizzas every day!

FASHIONABLE LADIES PESTS
INTELLIGENT DOMESTIC

Rats in the wild can be _____ . But _____ rats can be great pets. They are social and _____ . In the 1800s, rats were _____ pets for grand _____ .

Before getting a pet rat, you need to figure out how much it will cost. Do the math to complete this chart.

Item	Cost	How Often	Cost Per Year
Cage	$45	Once	
Bedding	$14	Every 3 months	
4 lbs (2 kg) of food	$8	Every month	
Food bowl	$3	Once	
Water bottle	$5	Once	
Chew toys	$4	Every month	
Care booklet	$5*	Once	
			TOTAL:

*You might find this book free at your local library!

Help this pet rat find his food and water.

Rats use their hair to find their way. Long whiskers on their faces and fine hairs in their coats allow them to feel their way around in the dark. Rats like to stay close to walls while moving around and rarely cross open spaces.

After traveling several times, rats "remember" their way with their muscles. If they get used to moving around an object, they will still travel around that spot even if that object is moved out of their way.

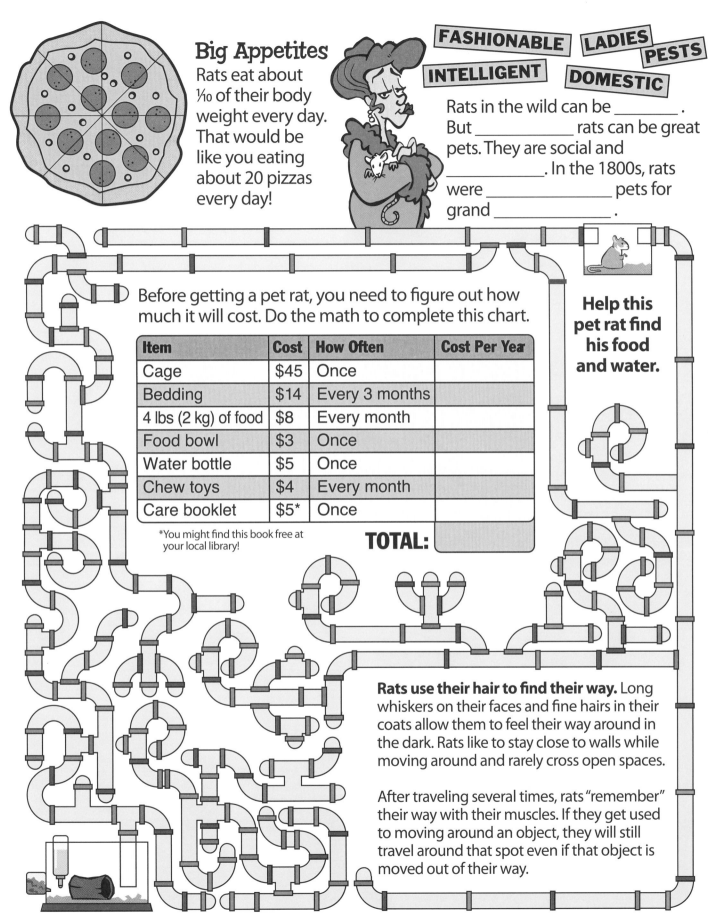

Top of the World

Reindeer live in the coldest part of the earth – not just at the North Pole, but also in the uppermost parts of Asia, Europe, and North America, that together are known as the Arctic Circle.

Find the two identical reindeer. Look very closely!

Draw a line to connect each title to the paragraph that matches it best.

A Step Ahead

Hollow Hairs

Moss Munchers

Reindeer mostly eat tough grass and a type of moss called **lichen**. It is easy for reindeer to eat during the summer, when new plants are growing, but it gets more difficult in winter. Luckily, their sharp hooves help them dig down through the snow and ice to reach the food they need.

Have you ever walked in deep snow? You take a step and sink. Reindeer have special hooves to help them walk on the snow and ice. Much like snowshoes, their hooves are wide, allowing them to walk on top of the snow without sinking.

A reindeer has a very thick coat of fur, which helps it survive the extreme cold of the Arctic Circle. Each hair in the coat is actually *hollow*. The animal's body heat warms up the air inside each hair, keeping the reindeer nice and toasty.

Reindeer Words
Do the math to match each word with its meaning.

Male reindeer: _____ (14)

Female reindeer: _____ (19)

Baby reindeer: _____ (13)

Group of reindeer: _____ (15)

Sound they make: _____ (16)

Reindeer love carrots! How many can you find on this page?

8 + 8 = BELLOW

9 + 3 + 3 = HERD

7 + 9 - 2 = BUCK

7 + 9 - 3 = FAWN

24 - 5 = DOE

Pulling Santa's Sleigh?

The tradition of reindeer pulling Santa's sleigh was first recognized by Clement C. Moore in his famous poem. Use the code to discover the name of Moore's poem that was first published in 1823.

```
1 = A
2 = C
3 = E
4 = H
5 = I
6 = O
7 = S
8 = T
9 = U
```

'W_ _ _ _ _
 8   17 843

N_G_ _ B_F_R_
 5 48   3 63

 _R_ _ _M_
 24 578   17

47

RHINOCEROSES

Mud Is Cool!

Rhino skin may look tough, but it's actually very sensitive. Rhinos can suffer from sunburn. To protect their skin from the sun and biting insects, a rhino will cover its skin in a thick layer of mud. Plus, that cool mud feels really good on hot days.

One Horn or Two?

There are five kinds of rhinos: black, white, Sumatran, Javan, and Indian. Javan and Indian rhinos have only one horn. Sumatran, black, and white rhinos have two.

What's in a Name?

Rhinos get their name from their most famous body part – their horns. The word *rhinoceros* comes from the Greek words *rhino* (nose) and *ceros* (horn).

Big Babies

Rhinos give birth to one calf at a time, which weighs over 100 pounds (45 kg)!

START

FINISH

Find the differences.

Charging into Trees?

Because their eyesight is rather poor, rhinos have been seen charging at boulders and trees that they mistake for attackers. This behavior has given rhinos a reputation for having a bad temper, but they are generally pretty mellow creatures.

Q: What do rhinos eat?

A: They use their horns to dig up roots and break branches, not for fighting. They are

▼ ⊡ ◧ ◿ ◪ ◩ ◨ ◧ ⊡ ◮

Use the Rhino Secret Code!

◣ = B ▼ = H ◤ = O ◮ = S

⊡ = E ◿ = I ◧ = R ◺ = V

Bird Buddies

The oxpecker is a bird seen perched on rhinos. They eat ticks and bugs that crawl around a rhino's skin, ears, and eyes. Such a relief!

Replace the missing words.

PAINTINGS SHAGGY MAMMAL ANCESTORS CHANCE EXISTED MILLION LONG HUNTING

Rhinos have been around for a very _____ time. Some scientists say they have been around for more than 50 _____ years!

Early rhinos had thick, _____ coats. Drawings of rhinos have been found in 30,000-year-old cave _____.

One of the rhinoceros's earliest _____, called the

paraceratherium, was 25 feet (8 m) long and 18 feet (6 m) high at the shoulder. It is regarded as the largest land _____ ever known.

Over the years, close to 100 rhinoceros species _____. Today, only five species continue the line: two native to Africa and three native to Asia. And due to overhunting, three of those five

species of rhinoceros are now Critically Endangered. That means they have a 50% _____ of becoming extinct.

The main reason that rhinos are endangered is due to illegal _____. Some people believe that rhinoceros horns can cure illnesses in humans, but there is no scientific evidence of that being true.

SEA OTTERS

Replace the missing words.

DENSEST
AMOUNT
COLD
COVER
DIRTY
OCEAN

Otter Appetite

Each day, a sea otter eats about one-fourth of its own body weight in food. That would be like:

a 60-pound person eating
5 + 5 + 5 = _____
pounds of food in one day.

a 100-pound person eating
10 + 12 + 3 = _____
pounds of food in one day.

a 148-pound person eating
15 + 17 + 5 = _____
pounds of food in one day.

Do the math to find out how many pounds of food each person would eat if he or she were a sea otter!

Fabulous Fur

Sea otters have very little body fat and rely on their fur to keep them warm in the cold Pacific _____ . Their fur is thick, perhaps the _____ in the world. If you were to put a penny on a sea otter, it would _____ about 250,000 hairs. That's more than twice the _____ of hair on your entire head!

Otter fur holds tiny air bubbles, which serve as insulation against the _____ .

If a sea otter's fur gets _____ , it won't hold air as well. Otters clean themselves often so that their fur can do its job.

Food Rocks!

Sea otters eat a lot of food every day. They eat crabs, clams, and red sea urchins.

Cracking the hard shells of these animals is tough, but the sea otter has found a solution. It is one of the few animals to use a tool.

A hungry sea otter finds a rock on the sea floor, tucks it beneath a flap of loose skin under a forelimb, grabs a few clams, and swims to the surface. It floats on its back and places the rock on its chest. It bangs a clam against the rock until it breaks open. Then the sea otter scoops out and eats the morsel of meat.

Circle what should come next in each row to continue the pattern.

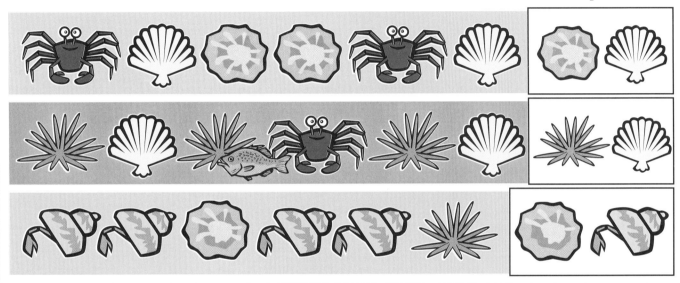

Oodles of Fun!

Sea otters spend a lot of time swimming and hunting for food, but still have plenty of time for play. Watching a sea otter at play brings a smile to nearly anyone's face.

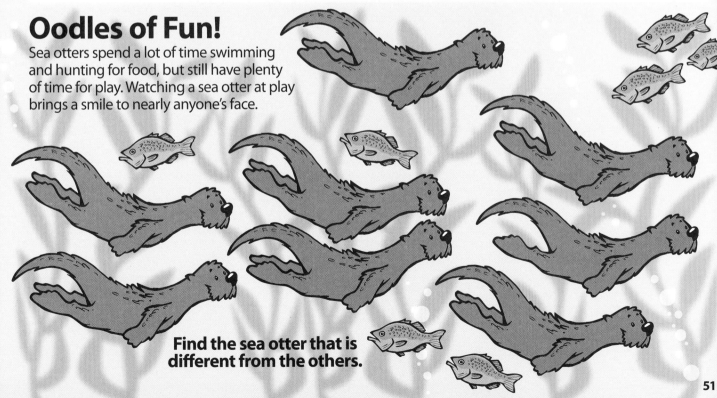

Find the sea otter that is different from the others.

STRANGE AND BEAUTIFUL
SEAHORSES

Can you find the two identical seahorses on this page?

Whoa, Nellie!

The seahorse looks like it is made up of many different animals. Unscramble each word below to find out the odd parts of the tiny seahorse.

A seahorse has:

The head and neck of a **soreh**.

The eyes of a **lachoenme**.
_ _ _ _ _ _ _ _ _

The pouch of a **noagrako**.
_ _ _ _ _ _ _ _

The tail of a **yonkem**.
_ _ _ _ _ _ _

The armor of an **liadamrol**.
_ _ _ _ _ _ _ _ _

This relative of the seahorse is a master of camouflage – blending in with its environment. Use the code to discover its name.

A D E G N O R S W Y

Tail Tale

A seahorse's tail is like a monkey's tail. Scientists call these **prehensile** tails because they can grasp like a hand. The seahorse's tail helps it to hang onto sea plants while it waits for food to swim by. Seahorses also hang onto each other with their tails.

Tiny and Toothless

The long snout of a seahorse gives the animal its horsey appearance. Unlike a horse, the seahorse's mouth does not open and close or have any teeth. The seahorse uses its snout like a little vacuum cleaner, sucking up its favorite food of brine shrimp, baby eels, and other tiny sea creatures.

What a Dad!

For most animals, the female of the species carries the young. Not so with the strange little seahorse.

When the female is ready to lay her eggs, she wraps her tail around a male seahorse's neck. Then, she deposits her eggs into a special pouch on the male seahorse's abdomen. The eggs hatch and grow inside this little pouch and the male's midsection gets very round and big.

When the little seahorses are big enough, the pouch starts to contract, and the baby seahorses are pushed into the wide, watery world.

Number the pictures in order to show how baby seahorses develop.

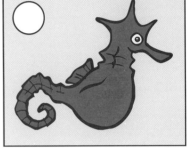

Wild Eyes

One seahorse eye can look up while the other looks down. One eye can look for food while the other is on the lookout for predators. Another kind of animal that has eyes that can move independently is the chameleon.

Help this seahorse escape the hungry fish!

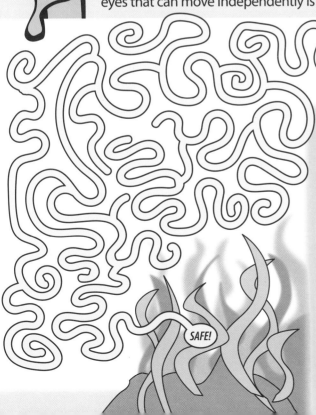

SAFE!

What kind of animal is a seahorse?

Take a guess, then color each box with an EVEN number BLUE and each with an ODD number RED to discover the answer. Did you guess correctly?

8	4	6	8	2	3	6	7	4	8	6	2	2	5	6	7	9	2
4	9	3	7	5	3	2	9	6	7	9	1	9	3	2	1	5	6
8	1	5	9	1	3	8	1	8	5	9	5	3	1	8	3	7	8
2	4	8	4	5	9	4	3	6	4	2	8	4	3	6	2	6	4
6	1	9	5	9	3	8	5	9	7	5	9	2	5	6	7	9	8
8	7	5	3	7	9	2	1	3	5	7	9	8	7	2	3	5	6
4	1	3	5	3	5	4	9	7	3	7	1	2	9	6	9	7	4
2	7	9	3	1	5	6	5	2	8	2	8	4	3	8	5	7	6

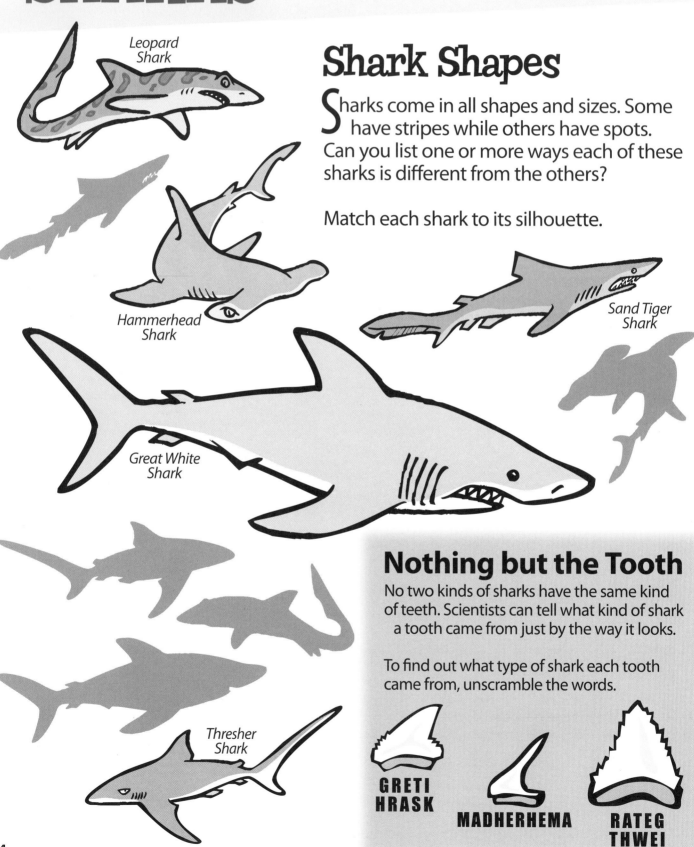

Leopard Shark

Hammerhead Shark

Sand Tiger Shark

Great White Shark

Thresher Shark

Shark Shapes

Sharks come in all shapes and sizes. Some have stripes while others have spots. Can you list one or more ways each of these sharks is different from the others?

Match each shark to its silhouette.

Nothing but the Tooth

No two kinds of sharks have the same kind of teeth. Scientists can tell what kind of shark a tooth came from just by the way it looks.

To find out what type of shark each tooth came from, unscramble the words.

GRETI HRASK

MADHERHEMA

RATEG THWEI

How Sharks Float

Shark livers are full of oil. To find out how oil helps sharks float, try this experiment.

STUFF YOU'LL NEED:

 JAR  SPOON   WATER  OIL

1. Put two tablespoons of cooking oil in a small jar.

2. Fill the jar halfway with water. Put the lid on the jar.

3. Shake the jar.

4. Set the jar down and watch what happens to the oil and water.

WRITE YOUR OBSERVATIONS HERE:

_____
_____
_____
_____

Most of the 300 species of sharks are not dangerous. In fact, **mosquitoes** are far more hazardous to humans than sharks!

Shark Teeth

Use this code to find out more amazing facts about shark teeth.

0   1   2   3   4

Most sharks have rows of teeth.

Sharks get a new set of teeth every weeks.

In 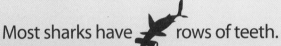 years, a tiger shark will lose

as many as  teeth.

Find the words in the puzzle by looking backwards, forwards, sideways, and diagonally.

```
F D A E H R E M M A H N J
R I B G R E Y R G N U H T
O D N C N H D Z E Y O L H
T E E T H S L L I G M I S
A E L Z O E B T X O I A I
D P Y W C R S A U H W T F
E K A K E H Q L S L S W E
R J S D A T O J V E T I B
P M V W N L E O P A R D F
```

FIN
TEETH
FISH
OCEAN
PREDATOR
JAW
DEEP
SWIM

HAMMERHEAD
TIGER
BITE
TAIL
LEOPARD
THRESHER
HUNGRY
GILLS

SNAILS

ONE FINE FOOT: Snails slide along the flat part of their body, called the "foot." Snails make a trail of silvery slime. This helps them to slide up walls and even crawl upside down.

THE SHELL: Snails hatch from eggs as teeny, tiny snails with a shell. As they grow, the shell grows and hardens.

The Beautiful Snail

Snails don't just live in gardens. They can also be found in ponds and even in the ocean. They are related to oysters, clams, and octopuses. Snails are part of the group of animals with soft bodies known as **mollusks**.

TENTACLE EYES AND NOSES: A snail's eyes are at the end of its long tentacles. The short tentacles are for smelling.

BREATHING HOLE: Snails breathe through a hole near their shell.

The Great Snail Race

Draw a large circle on a piece of paper. Draw a small circle inside the large circle.

Find two or more snails and put them in the small circle. Watch to see which one slides out to the large circle first. Be gentle and return the snail to the place you found it. Then wash your hands.

Do the math to see which of these snails will win the race. Highest number wins!

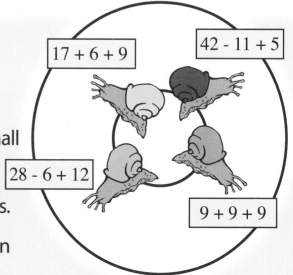

17 + 6 + 9

42 - 11 + 5

28 - 6 + 12

9 + 9 + 9

Make a ...

SNAIL MOTEL
VACANCY

You can make a comfy motel and invite some snails for a visit. Look for snail travelers under rocks and leaves.

1. Partially fill a large jar with moist soil.

2. Add a piece of chalk, some leaves, grass, and chunks of bark.

3. Give the snails lettuce and cabbage leaves to eat.

4. Keep the jar covered with a piece of nylon stocking or window screen.

5. Keep the Snail Motel in a shady place.

6. Twice a week replace the old soil and food.

Help this snail find its way to the Snail Motel.

If the weather turns very cold or very dry, a snail pulls into its shell and waits for the cool, damp weather it loves. It fills up the opening of its shell with a mucas-like slime that hardens into a snug door.

The snail has a Latin name that means "a belly-footed animal." Use the code to find out what this name is.

A = ●   G = ◥◣   O = ■   S = ✚
D = ▲   H = ☽   P = ★   T = ⚡
F = ▣   N = ▼   R = ☾   U = ➤

SNAKES

Slither Power

Moving around without arms or legs is no problem for snakes. That's because they've developed several ways to move. Here are two:

Concertina

The snake scrunches up its body like an accordian or *concertina*. First it loops then straightens out, pushing its head forward. Then it pulls its tail along and starts again.

① ② ③

Creeping

Some snakes can slide back and forth, gripping the ground with their belly scales.

When a snake is creeping, its body is almost straight.

The Anaconda

The anaconda is one large snake. They can grow as long as a school bus! Add the numbers on this anaconda to discover how many feet long the largest one on record is.

Anacondas wait near the water's edge. When an unlucky critter comes by, the anaconda winds itself around its prey, dragging it into the water and holding it underwater until it drowns. Then the anaconda swallows the animal **whole!** After a meal, an anaconda will rest for one whole week.

Look closely. Which snake has a different pattern than all the others?

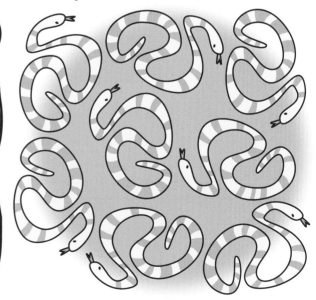

Help this little desert mouse make its way through the rattlers!

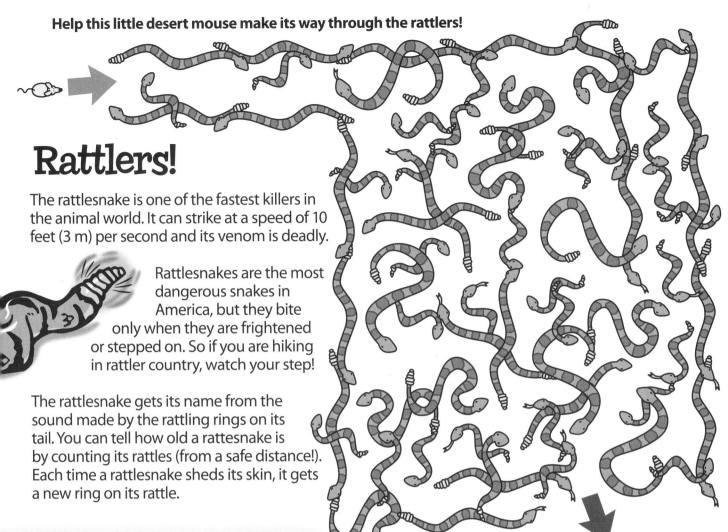

Rattlers!

The rattlesnake is one of the fastest killers in the animal world. It can strike at a speed of 10 feet (3 m) per second and its venom is deadly.

Rattlesnakes are the most dangerous snakes in America, but they bite only when they are frightened or stepped on. So if you are hiking in rattler country, watch your step!

The rattlesnake gets its name from the sound made by the rattling rings on its tail. You can tell how old a rattesnake is by counting its rattles (from a safe distance!). Each time a rattlesnake sheds its skin, it gets a new ring on its rattle.

UNSCRAMBLE IT!

Q: Snakes never blink. Why?
A: They have no YEEDISL.

_ _ _ _ _ _ _ _

Q: How do snakes avoid their enemies?
A: By smelling or "tasting" the air with their ROKFED GONUET.

_ _ _ _ _ _   _ _ _ _ _ _

The cobra is one of the most poisonous snakes. A bite from a cobra can kill a person in 🦴➕ minutes. Cobras can bite and kill as soon as they are born.

Just one tablespoon of their venom could kill 🦴◯➕ people!

Cobra Secret Code

🦴 =1   🐍 =3   ➕ =5

◯ =6   🐍 =8

TARANTULAS

Hairy and Scary

The Goliath bird-eating tarantula is the biggest spider on the planet. It's so big that it could cover your entire face!

It is also the hairiest tarantula. But is it the scariest?

Some people think so. But the reality is that no one has ever died from a tarantula bite. Tarantulas really don't want to bite people. They only attack what they want to eat.

How many tarantulas can you find on this page?

How a Tarantula Eats

Replace the missing words.

TOSSES   BITES   TURNS   FLUID

First the tarantula _____ and paralyzes its prey. Then it pumps _____ from its stomach into its intended meal. The stomach fluid _____ the inside of the prey to liquid. The spider then slurps the liquid and _____ the skin away.

Most spiders only live a season or two. That's not the case for tarantulas. Some can live 12 + 9 + 9 = _____ years!

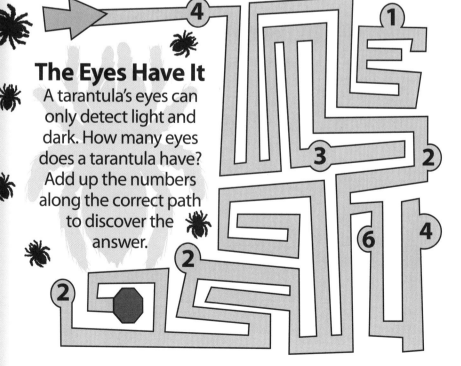

The Eyes Have It

A tarantula's eyes can only detect light and dark. How many eyes does a tarantula have? Add up the numbers along the correct path to discover the answer.

Leg Redo

If a tarantula loses a leg, it can grow a new one. In fact, a tarantula will chew off and eat its own injured leg in order to get a new, healthy leg.

Yum!

Tarantula-Eating People

While tarantulas don't eat people, some people eat tarantulas. People in the jungles of French Guiana like to roast and eat these spiders. Sometimes, they even use the tarantula's fangs as toothpicks after their meal!

Find the twin tarantulas.

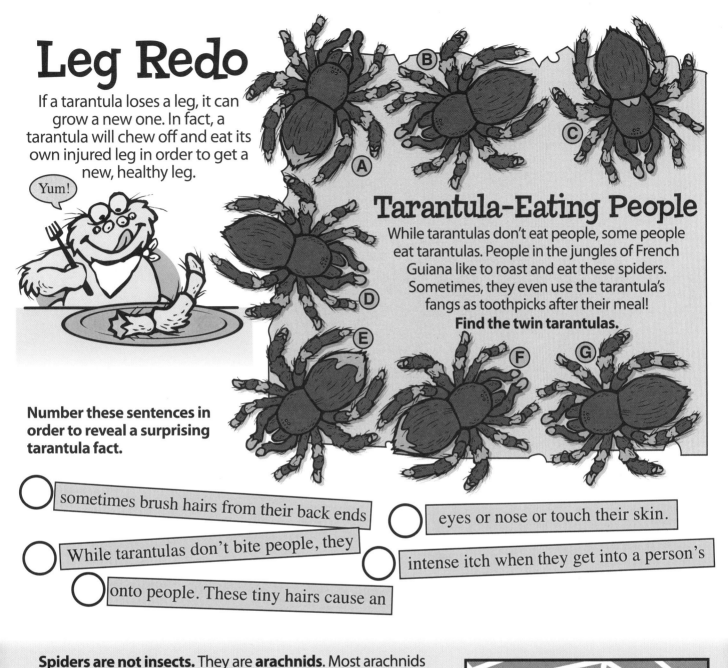

Number these sentences in order to reveal a surprising tarantula fact.

◯ sometimes brush hairs from their back ends

◯ While tarantulas don't bite people, they

◯ onto people. These tiny hairs cause an

◯ eyes or nose or touch their skin.

◯ intense itch when they get into a person's

Spiders are not insects. They are **arachnids**. Most arachnids have four pairs of legs. Arachnids do not have antennae. Use the code to discover other members of the arachnid family.

SECRET CODE

◩ = C ⬚ = E ⊠ = I ⊻ = K ◺ = M ⊟ = N
◿ = O ⊟ = P ◖ = R ⊟ = S ◈ = T ◗ = U

How do you spot a modern spider?

ANSWER: By its website.

LARGEST OF THE CATS
TIGERS

Find your way through the tiger's stripes.

Making a Splash

Tigers are one of the few members of the cat family that love to swim. They're good swimmers and will plunge into rivers and streams to cool off.

Dinner Time

Tigers hunt alone. They kill their prey with a bite to the neck. A tiger will eat until full, then cover its meal with dirt and leaves and return to it later when it's hungry again.

Singular Stripes

Every tiger has stripes that are unique to that individual tiger, so no two tigers are the same. There are more than 100 stripes on a tiger.

The average tiger weighs about 450 pounds (204 kg) – heavier than a piano!

Tiger Trivia Trail

2. Tigers can jump up to 33 feet (10 m) in a single leap.
☐ TRUE ☐ FALSE

1. All tigers have white spots on the back of their ears.
☐ TRUE ☐ FALSE

4. A tiger's roar can be heard 5 miles (8 km) away.
☐ TRUE ☐ FALSE

5. Tigers' paw prints are called pug marks.
☐ TRUE
☐ FALSE

3. Tigers hate to get wet.
☐ TRUE ☐ FALSE

Siberian Tigers

The Siberian tiger lives in the icy northern lands of Siberia. Its fur is a light yellow-brown color and it has fewer stripes than other tigers.

Siberian tiger   **Bengal tiger**

Hunting and loss of habitat greatly decreased the Siberian tiger population. In 1981, there were only about 150 Siberian tigers left. Today, the number of Siberian tigers in the wild is around 500, thanks to protection programs.

If an African lion fought an African tiger, who would win?

Replace the missing vowels.

N _ _ TH _ R.
TH _ R _ ARE
N _
T _ G _ RS
IN AFR _ C _ .

Replace the missing words.

LION   YAWN   FAMILY   JAW   CAT

Often people call a large prehistoric _____ with two long, curving upper teeth a **saber-toothed tiger**. However, this extinct cat didn't belong to the tiger _____. Scientists call this saber-toothed cat a *Smilodon*.

The Smilodon lived only in the Americas. It was a little shorter than a modern-day African _____, but heavier. Its _____ opened to a gaping 95-degree angle or more! The widest _____ of a lion today is only about a 65-degree angle.

Look closely: Only two of these tiger tails are exactly the same.

A   B   C   D   E   F   G   H

ANSWERS

Page 8

R B A T R P J S P V W L T D E Z A S
APPLES

P E O C D N M G I K A O Y W N K L S
ONIONS

W U P G H U L B M I O P J T K S D I L Y N O K S
PUMPKINS

S I C H I H M B E W V R T S R Z Q I P L E A F S
CHERRIES

Page 9

How many bees can you find?
67

Flowers grid:
3 6 3 7
0 4 2 5
5 3 6 0
2 1 0 2

Page 10

A N T A R C T I C A
B O U B S D U J D B

A butterfly can fly at a top speed of:
12 mph (19 kph)

Page 11

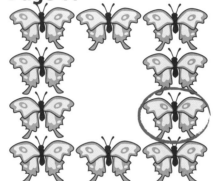

Flight of the Monarch
While quite small, the beautiful **ORANGE** and black monarch butterfly makes one of the longest migrations in the animal **KINGDOM**.

Monarch butterflies live in Canada and the northern part of the United States in the spring and summer. Every fall, when the weather turns **COLD**, millions of monarch butterflies begin flying **SOUTH** to southern California and central Mexico.

The butterflies **RETURN** to the same forests each year, and some even find the same tree where their parents and grandparents wintered.

Scientists aren't sure how the monarchs know where to go each year, since they each only make the trip **ONCE**.

Page 12

9,500
The number of years ago that we believe cats were first tamed.

2 9 5
MILLION
The approximate number of dollars spent each year in the U.S. for kitty litter.

35,000
The approximate number of kittens born in the U.S. each day.

3 2
The number of muscles in each ear of a cat.

Page 12

Cat Prints
NOSE

Page 13

How many mice can you find?
17

Page 14

Page 14

H	O	W	L	S
W	L	H	S	O
L	H	S	O	W
S	W	O	H	L
O	S	L	W	H

Page 15

Coyote Code

Coyotes can jump over **13** feet (4 m). That's higher than a basketball hoop, which is **10** feet (3 m) above the ground.

A coyote litter can have **3** to **12** pups.

Coyotes can run over **40** miles per hour (64 kph).

Coyotes live about **14** years in the wild.

Coyotes can make **11** different sounds.

Page 16

How do crocodiles sweat?

They sweat through their mouths

Page 17

Mirror Fact

Crocodiles swallow stones to help them digest their food.

Pool of Facts

The largest recorded alligator: **19** feet (5.8 m) long.

The largest recorded crocodile: **28** feet (8.5 m) long.

Alligators have **70** to **80** teeth. They grow new ones to replace broken teeth. One alligator can have as many as **2,000** teeth in a lifetime!

Page 17

Crocs can stay underwater for **15** to **20** minutes. They close their nostrils when they swim underwater.

LOUISIANA
IOLASUANI
FLORIDA
ODARLIF

Page 18
How many bones do you see?
16

Page 19

Relax, pal! I was just taking a nap!

Name That Breed
1: Labrador Retriever
2: German Shepherd
3: Poodle

Page 20

African Elephants

African elephants are **LARGER** than Asian elephants. They have large ears shaped a little like the continent of **AFRICA**. Large ears help keep the elephant **COOL** on the **HOT** African plains. African elephants have a swayback and very **WRINKLED** skin. They also have a rounded head without any bumps.

Page 20

Asian Elephants

Asian elephants live in **COOLER** forest areas and they have **SMALLER** ears. They also have rounded **BACKS**, smoother skin, and a **HIGH** forehead with two "bumps." Asian elephants can **EAT** more than 300 pounds (136 kg) of grass, leaves, and plant material every day.

Page 21

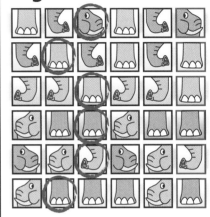

Trunk Truths

#3 is false. There are no bones in an elephant's trunk.

Page 22
How Many Bones Are in a Giraffe's Neck?
Giraffe neck = 7
Human neck = 7

Tongue Twister
22 inches (56 cm)

Page 23

Page 23

How tall is a giraffe?

$2 + 16 = 18$ feet (5.5 m)

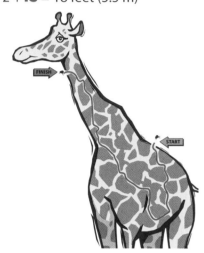

Page 24

Gorilla Troops

Gorillas like to be around other gorillas, so they live in **GROUPS**, called troops, as one big gorilla family. A troop can **INCLUDE** more than 30 gorillas, led by one or more silverback gorillas. These leaders **DECIDE** where the troop will live, and when it will wake up, **EAT**, and go back to bed. They also make sure that no troop member **HURTS** another.

Page 25

$23 + 11 + 11 = 45$

$7 + 9 - 4 = 12$

$8 + 4 = 12$

$19 - 8 = 11$

$18 + 18 + 9 = 45$

$12 + 24 + 9 = 45$

$28 - 19 = 9$

Page 26

(A) antennae, used to feel, smell, and taste

(B) small legs to hold body at shell opening

(C) front claws

(D) abdomen

(E) eyestalks

(F) walking legs, two on each side

$4 + 13 + 8 = 25$

$11 + 6 + 2 = 19$

$3 + 5 + 5 = 13$

$9 + 5 + 3 = 17$

$6 + 4 + 2 = 12$

$3 + 3 + 3 = 9$

$7 + 9 + 5 = 21$

Page 27

Page 28

Page 28

Hungry, Hungry Hummingbirds
Bananas

Use the code to learn more about hummingbirds.

The ruby-throated hummingbird weighs less than a **PENNY**

The smallest hummingbird lives in Peru and is the size of a **BEE**

Do hummingbirds hum? Yes! Their wings make a faint humming sound when they are **FLYING**

Page 29

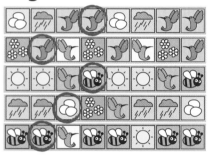

How many hummingbirds and flowers can you find?
28 hummingbirds
59 flowers

Fluttering Facts
Hummingbirds are the only birds that can fly in any **DIRECTION**: forward, backward, up, down, and side-to-side.

Hummingbirds pollinate flowers because **POLLEN** sticks to their wings. This feeding behavior is vital to helping **FLOWERS** become pollinated, which makes hummingbirds very important to the ecosystem.

Page 29

During migration, ruby-throated hummingbirds fly nonstop over the Gulf of Mexico – it can take up to 22 hours of **CONTINUOUS** flight over 500 miles (805 km) of water. The rufous hummingbird has the longest migration, traveling up to 6,000 miles (9,700 km) from its winter home to its **SUMMER** breeding grounds.

Hummingbirds' nests and eggs are tiny. The eggs are about the size of **JELLY BEANS**. The nest is about the size of a walnut.

Page 30

Roo Features

A kangaroo, or roo, has **LARGE** back legs, small front legs, and a head shaped like that of a deer. Its well-developed **SENSES** include excellent scanning eyesight and sharp **HEARING** provided by large rabbit-like ears that can turn frontward or back. In a larger roo, the tail acts as a **SUPPORT** for sitting, but also helps the animal **STEER** when hopping. Powerful back legs propel larger roos to speeds of up to 40 mph (64 kph).

Page 31

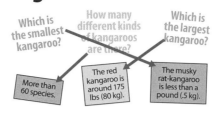

What do you call groups of kangaroos?
Mobs

What do you call a kangaroo that weighs less than 45 lbs (20 kg)?
Wallaby

What do you call a baby kangaroo?
Joey

Page 32

Page 33

Koala Code

Koalas eat about **3** pounds (1 kg) of leaves every day. That's about **21**% of a koala's weight.

In the wild, koalas live about **31** years.

Koalas sleep about **18** hours a day.

An adult koala weighs about **31** pounds (14 kg).

Page 33

Feet Made for Tree Climbing

A koala's claws are just right for **HOLDING** onto tree trunks and branches. The front paws have five toes: two on one side of the foot and three on the other. That's like having two thumbs, an arrangement that gives the koala a strong **GRIP**.

The toes on the back paws are different from those on the front. In back, there's a **ROUND** "big toe" without a claw, plus three other toes, two of which are joined to form one digit with two claws. These joined toes are **USED** for grooming.

Page 34

Page 34

Lion cubs have spots.
TRUE

In the wild, lions can go a week without eating.
TRUE

Lions have five legs.
FALSE

Lions are herbivores.
FALSE

A full-grown lion can eat 75 pounds (34 kg) of meat at one time.
TRUE

A group of lions is called a pride.
TRUE

Page 35

Hide and Seek
16 cubs

Look-Alike Lions
C and G

Page 37

How many fish can you find?
40

Page 37

Page 38

Page 39

Page 39

Orcas are warm-blooded.
TRUE

Orcas lay eggs.
FALSE

Orcas feed milk to their babies.
TRUE

Orcas have scales.
FALSE

Orcas give birth to live young.
TRUE

Orcas have hair.
FALSE

Page 40

Always Hungry
22 pounds (10 kg)

Page 41

Endangered Pandas
World Wildlife Fund

How many pandas can you find?
43

Where to See Pandas
San Diego Zoo: **3**
Smithsonian National Zoo: **4**
Memphis Zoo: **2**
Toronto Zoo: **2**
Zoo Atlanta: **4**

Page 42

How Polar Bears Stay Warm
Fat and Fur

Page 43

Polar Bear True or False
All **TRUE**

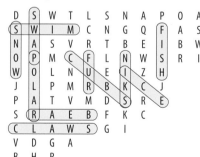

What's another name for a polar bear's layer of fat?
BLUBBER

Page 44
Rats Have Expensive Taste
From the day it is born, a rat's **TEETH** never stop growing. They can grow up to five **INCHES** a year. Rats must continue to **GNAW** on hard surfaces to wear down their teeth or they will **DIE**.

Rats can chew through walls, **WIRING**, plastic, and more. It is estimated that rats **CAUSE** about $20 billion in damage to homes, **FARMS**, and businesses in the United States each year.

Rats can bite down with a force of 7,000 pounds per square inch. That's about the same force as a crocodile's bite!

Page 45
Rats in the wild can be **PESTS**. But **DOMESTIC** rats can be great pets. They are social and **INTELLIGENT**. In the 1800s, rats were **FASHIONABLE** pets for grand **LADIES**.

Item	Cost	How Often	Cost Per Year
Cage	$45	Once	**$45**
Bedding	$14	Every 3 months	**$56**
4 lbs (2 kg) of food	$8	Every month	**$96**
Food bowl	$3	Once	**$3**
Water bottle	$5	Once	**$5**
Chew toys	$4	Every month	**$48**
Care booklet	$5*	Once	**$5**
		TOTAL:	**$258**

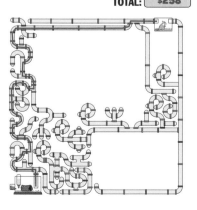

Page 46
Find the two identical reindeer.
C and E

Page 47

How many carrots can you find?
19

Reindeer Words
Male reindeer: **BUCK**
Female reindeer: **DOE**
Baby reindeer: **FAWN**
Group of reindeer: **HERD**
Sound they make: **BELLOW**

Pulling Santa's Sleigh
'Twas the Night Before Christmas

Page 48

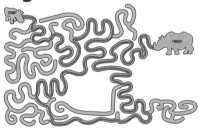

Page 49
Replace the missing words.
Rhinos have been around for a very **LONG** time. Some scientists say they have been around for more than 50 **MILLION** years!

Early rhinos had thick, **SHAGGY** coats. Drawings of rhinos have been found in 30,000-year-old cave **PAINTINGS**.

One of the rhinoceros's earliest **ANCESTORS**, called the *paracer-atherium*, was 25 feet (8 m) long and 18 feet (6 m) high at the shoulder. It is regarded as the largest land **MAMMAL** ever known.

Page 49
Over the years, close to 100 rhinoceros species **EXISTED**. Today, only five species continue the line: two native to Africa and three native to Asia. And due to overhunting, three of those five species of rhinoceros are now Critically Endangered. That means they have a 50% **CHANCE** of becoming extinct.

The main reason that rhinos are endangered is due to illegal **HUNTING**. Some people believe that rhinoceros horns can cure illnesses in humans, but there is no scientific evidence of that being true.

What do rhinos eat?
They are **HERBIVORES**

Page 50
Fabulous Fur
Sea otters have very little body fat and rely on their fur to keep them warm in the cold Pacific **OCEAN**. Their fur is thick, perhaps the **DENSEST** in the world. If you were to put a penny on a sea otter, it would **COVER** about 250,000 hairs. That's more than twice the **AMOUNT** of hair on your entire head!

Page 50

Otter fur holds tiny air bubbles, which serve as insulation against the **COLD**.

If a sea otter's fur gets **DIRTY**, it won't hold air as well. Otters clean themselves often so that their fur can do its job.

Otter Appetite
a 60-pound person eating **15** pounds (7 kg) of food in one day.

a 100-pound person eating **25** pounds (11 kg) of food in one day.

a 148-pound person eating **37** pounds (17 kg) of food in one day.

Page 51

Page 52

Can you find the two identical seahorses on this page?
C and H

A seahorse has:
The head and neck of a horse.
The eyes of a chameleon.
The pouch of a kangaroo.
The tail of a monkey.
The armor of an armadillo.

Page 52

WEEDY
SEA
DRAGON

Page 53

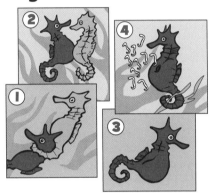

Page 54

TIGER SHARK   HAMMERHEAD   GREAT WHITE

Page 55

Shark Teeth
Most sharks have **4** rows of teeth.
Sharks get a new set of teeth every **2** weeks.
In **10** years, a tiger shark will lose as many as **24,000** teeth.

Page 55

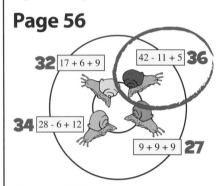

Page 56

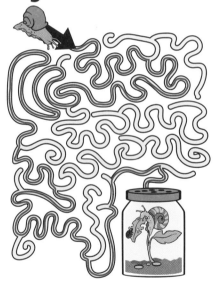

32 17 + 6 + 9   42 − 11 + 5 **36**

34 28 − 6 + 12

9 + 9 + 9 **27**

Page 57

GASTROPOD

Page 58

The Anaconda
33 ft (10 m)

Page 58

Page 59

Snakes never blink. Why?
They have no **EYELIDS**.

How do snakes avoid their enemies?
By smelling or "tasting" the air with their **FORKED TONGUE**.

Cobra Secret Code
The cobra is one of the most poisonous snakes. A bite from a cobra can kill a person in **15** minutes. Cobras can bite and kill as soon as they are born. Just one tablespoon of their venom could kill **165** people!

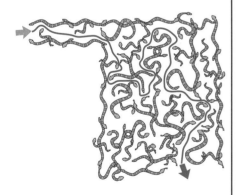

Page 60

How many tarantulas can you find?
24

How a Tarantula Eats
First the tarantula **BITES** and paralyzes its prey. Then it pumps **FLUID** from its stomach into its intended meal. The stomach fluid **TURNS** the inside of the prey to liquid. The spider then slurps the liquid and **TOSSES** the skin away.

Most spiders only live a season or two. That's not the case for tarantulas. Some can live **30** years!

The Eyes Have It
8 eyes

Page 61

Find the twin tarantulas.
B and D

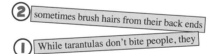

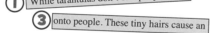

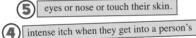

Page 62

Tiger Trivia Trail

1. True.

2. True.

3. False – tigers are good swimmers.

4. False, but a tiger's roar can be heard as much as 2 miles (3 km) away.

5. True.

Page 63

If an African lion fought an African tiger, who would win?

NEITHER. THERE ARE NO TIGERS IN AFRICA.

Replace the missing words.
Often people call a large prehistoric **CAT** with two long, curving upper teeth a **saber-toothed tiger**. However, this extinct cat didn't belong to the tiger **FAMILY**. Scientists call this saber-toothed cat a *Smilodon*.

The Smilodon lived only in the Americas. It was a little shorter than a modern-day African **LION**, but heavier. Its **JAW** opened to a gaping 95-degree angle or more! The widest **YAWN** of a lion today is only about a 65-degree angle.

Look closely: Only two of these tiger tails are exactly the same.
C and F

Who Made This Book?

Mind-Boggling Animal Puzzles was made by the people who bring the weekly *Kid Scoop* page to hundreds of newspapers!

Kid Scoop **believes learning is fun!** Our educational activity pages teach and entertain. Teachers use the page in schools to promote standards-based learning. Parents use the *Kid Scoop* materials to foster academic success, a joy of learning, and family discussions.

Over 25 years of experience in the field has taught us that children learn when they are engaged in the subject. We know that our puzzles and activities draw children into the page. This stimulates children's interest, and they then read the text.

When Fox Chapel Publishing discovered *Kid Scoop*, they knew that there were lots of kids looking for something just like this book!

Vicki Whiting – Author

Vicki was a third-grade teacher for many years. Now she loves teaching kids through the weekly entertaining and educational *Kid Scoop* page. People often ask where she gets her ideas for each week's page. Vicki says, "I listen to the questions kids ask. We answer those questions with every *Kid Scoop* page!"

Jeff Schinkel – Illustrator

Jeff has loved to draw his whole life! As a kid, sometimes he was drawing when he should have been listening to the teacher in class. That's when he knew he should go to art school, where he would want to hear everything the teachers had to say! Jeff attended the Academy of Art University in San Francisco and now he loves teaching kids how to draw.